Classroom Activities for Introductory Sociology Courses

Prepared by

Contributions from Instructors Around the Country

WADSWORTH
CENGAGE Learning

Australia • Brazil • Japan • Korea • Mexico • Singapore • Spain • United Kingdom • United States

Classroom Activities for Introductory Sociology Courses

For product information and technology assistance, contact us at **Cengage Learning Customer & Sales Support, 1-800-354-9706**

For permission to use material from this text or product, submit all requests online at **cengage.com/permissions** Further permissions questions can be emailed to **permissionrequest@cengage.com**

ISBN-13: 978-0-495-51045-1

ISBN-10: 0-495-51045-9

Wadsworth
10 Davis Drive
Belmont, CA 94002-3098
USA

Cengage Learning is a leading provider of customized learning solutions with office locations around the globe, including Singapore, the United Kingdom, Australia, Mexico, Brazil, and Japan. Locate your local office at: **international.cengage.com/region**

Cengage Learning products are represented in Canada by Nelson Education, Ltd.

For your course and learning solutions, visit **academic.cengage.com**

Purchase any of our products at your local college store or at our preferred online store **www.ichapters.com**

Printed in the United States of America
2 3 4 5 6   17 16 15 14 13

Table of Contents

Letter from the Editor   iv.
Form to Submit An Activity   v.
Index of Contributors   viii.

Topic 1   General Teaching Tactics   1
Topic 2   Sociological Perspectives   27
Topic 3   Research Methods   36
Topic 4   Culture   42
Topic 5   Socialization   46
Topic 6   Social Structure and Interaction   48
Topic 7   Groups and Organizations   54
Topic 8   Deviance and Crime   57
Topic 9   Class and Stratification   62
Topic 10   Race and Ethnicity   67
Topic 11   Sex and Gender   72
Topic 12   Aging and Age-Based Inequality   83
Topic 13   Politics and the Economy   85
Topic 14   Families/Intimate Relationships   88
Topic 15   Education and Religion   92
Topic 16   Health, Health Care, Disability   97
Topic 17   Population and Urbanization   99
Topic 18   Collective Behavior and Change   101

Dear Instructor,

I'm pleased to introduce *Lecture Ideas and Activities for Introductory Sociology,* a collection of classroom activities written by sociology instructors around the country. This idea came about when I asked textbook reviewers to answer the question, "Please describe either a classroom demonstration or teaching tactic that you use to make a topic fun or interesting for students." The responses were so creative and fun to read that I couldn't help thinking other professors would like to have access to them for use in their classrooms. So I asked their permission to publish them and began gathering more entries via an online survey. The result is the first edition of this little book, which I hope to revise every year.

I invite you to participate in the second edition by submitting an activity or idea that you think livens up your classroom. If we decide to include your activity in the next edition, you will receive a small compensation as well as the gratification that comes with knowing you've helped your colleagues who need some fresh ideas for their own marriage and family classes.

To share your ideas, email me at chris.caldeira@cengage.com or fill out the forms on the next few pages and mail it in. I look forward to reading your ideas!

Sincerely,
Chris Caldeira
Acquisitions Editor
Wadsworth Publishing
10 Davis Drive
Belmont, CA 94002

Do you have a Lecture Idea / Activity to share?

If you have a classroom activity that your students enjoy, consider publishing it in the next edition of *Lecture Ideas and Acitivities for Introductory Sociology*! You can e-mail or send the information on this form to Chris Caldeira, chris.caldeira@cengage.com.

> Chris Caldeira
> Acquisitions Editor
> Wadsworth /Cengage
> 10 Davis Drive
> Belmont, CA 94002

*Please note that this submission will potentially be published in the next (and subsequent) revisions of the booklet. If your submission is included, you will be listed as a contributor and receive a complimentary copy of Lecture Ideas for Courses on the Family *upon publication. We would also issue a small token of appreciation for contributing to this supplement's success.*

➢ Name
_____

➢ School affiliation
_____

➢ E-mail
_____

Please describe your creative classroom / lecture activity here in a ready-for-publication format, and with as much detail as possible:

_____
_____
_____
_____
_____

_____

_____

_____

_____

_____

_____

_____

➢ The Introductory Sociology course topic that this correlates to is _____.

➢ May we include your e-mail address in the booklet?
Yes / No (Circle One)

➢ Do you have an interest in writing supplementary materials?
Yes / No (Circle One)

Thank you for your input! These suggestions will be carefully considered by our editorial group for incorporation in our *Lecture Ideas* supplement.

IMPORTANT: Please complete the permissions form on the next page!
If your suggestion is submitted through e-mail, we will contact you electronically for the Permission to Publish.

Permission to Publish

I am granting permission for my activity to be published
in any and all revised versions of a supplement called
"Lecture Ideas for Courses on the Family" for
Cengage Learning Higher Education.

This permission in no way restricts publication of my
material in any form by me or by others authorized by
me. It is understood that Cengage Learning Higher Education
will not have the right to grant permission for third parties
to use this material as a separate item.

I (we) grant permission for the use outlined above.

_____

Name   Date

_____

Affiliation

_____

_____

_____

Address

Index of Contributors

Michael K. Abel, 42
Brigham Young
University-Idaho
abelm@byui.edu

**Jan AbuShakrah, 27, 48,
85, 92, 97**
Portland Comm. College
Andersen/Taylor's
Sociology: The Essentials
IRM

Janet S. Armitage, 1
St. Mary's University
jarmitage1@stmarytx.edu

David J. Ayers, 62, 92, 99
Grove City College
Stark Sociology IRM

Mark Bird, 1
College of Southern
Nevada
mark.bird@ccsn.edu

Shelley Brown, 83
Tennessee Technological
University
csbrown@tntech.edu

Shelly Brown-Jeffy, 2
University of North
Carolina at Greensboro
slbrown2@Uncg.edu

Tawny Brown-Warren, 4
Columbia College
tbrownwarren@cougars.
ccis.edu

Claudia Chaufan, 72
University of California
Santa Cruz
claudiachaufan@yahoo.
com

Janet Cosbey, 43
Eastern Illinois University
jrcosbey@eiu.edu

William M. Cross, 54
Illinois College
cross@ic.edu

LaKeisha Crye Green, 13
Delgado Community
College
lcrye@dcc.edu

Thom Curtis, 5
University of Hawaii
at Hilo
thomc@hawaii.edu

William Danaher, 5, 36
College of Charleston
danaherw@cofc.edu

Katheryn A. Dietrich, 93
Texas A&M University
Mooney/Knox/Schacht's
*Understanding Social
Problem*s IRMTB

Tracy L. Dietz, 44, 62
University of Central
Florida
Brinkerhoff's *Essentials of
Sociology* IRM

Monica Edwards, 74
Loyola University Chicago
medwar1@luc.edu

William J. Elenchin, 63
St. Bonaventure University
welenchi@sbu.edu

Maxine Elmont, 7
MassBay Community
College
Melmont@massbay.edu

Robin Ersing, 6
University of South Florida
rersing@cas.usf.edu

Joan Ferrante, 45
Northern Kentucky
University
Ferrante *Sociology: A
Global Perspective* 7e IRM

Ryan G. Fletcher, 8
Brookhaven College -
Dallas
rgfletch7@dcccd.edu

Patrick E. Fontane, 9
St. Louis College of
Pharmacy
pfontane@stlcop.edu

Kristie A. Ford, 10, 75
Skidmore College
kford@skidmore.edu

Lori Ann Fowler, 86
Tarrant County College
Study Guide for Mooney's
*Understanding Social
Problems*, 5E

Erik Fritsvold, 28
University of San Diego
erikf@sandiego.edu

Laura Garcia, 97
Washington State
Community College
lgarcia@wscc.edu

Robert Gellman, 78
Kansas State University
*Lecture Ideas for Courses
on the Family,* Vol 1, p. 25

Phil Gillette, 48
University of Maryland
University College -
Europe
pgillette@faculty.ed.umuc.
edu

Cristina Gordon, 64
Fox Valley Technical
College
gordon@fvtc.edu

Ron J. Hammond, 67
Utah Valley State College
IMTB for Marger's *Race
and Ethnic Relations,* 7E

Jill Harrison, 27, 36, 67
Rhode Island College
jharrison@ric.edu

Jeanne Humble, 48
Bluegrass Community and
Technical College
jshumb1@uky.edu

Hui M Huo, 13
Highline Community
College
hhuo@highline.edu

Dana Hysock, 78
University of Delaware
Andersen and Hill Collins's
*Race, Class, and Gender:
An Anthology,* IMTB 6E

Carolyn Irwin Burns, 43
Calhoun at Huntsville
irwin40328@aol.com

Shirley A. Jackson, 68
Southern Connecticut State
University
jacksons1@southernct.edu

**Caroll B. Johnson
Hodson, 57, 88, 101**
Rowan-Cabarrus
Community College
hodgsonc@rowancabarrus.
edu

Sharon Jones, 55
Belhaven College - Jackson
scjones@bellsouth.net

Diane C. Keithly, 37
Southern University
Dckeithly@AOL.com

Aiden Kenny, 14
County College of Morris
ajk33@ptonline.net

Grace Keyes, 14, 30
St. Mary's University
gkeyes@stmarytx.edu

David Knox, 84
East Carolina University
Knox *Choices in
Relationships* 9e IRM/TB

Maxwell N. Kwenda, 39
Cameron University
mkwenda@cameron.edu

William Kornblum, 55
City University of NY
Carolyn D. Smith
Study Guide for
Kornblum's *Sociology*, 8E

Carol LaLiberte, 49
Asnuntuck Community
College
clalib0254@aol.com

Gary R. Lemons, 16
Scottsdale Community
College
gary.lemons@sccmail.
maricopa.edu

**Timothy D. Levonyan
Radloff, 19**
SUNY Fredonia
levonyan@fredonia.edu

Alicia Lupinacci, 56
Tarrant County College
Northwest Campus
alicia.lupinacci@tccd.edu

Donald Malone, 79, 89
Saint Peter's College
dmalone@spc.edu

**Jerry Jo Manfred-
Gilham, 65**
Franciscan University of
Steubenville
jgilham@franciscan.edu

Etsuko Maruoka, 31, 33, 39, 80
Suffolk County
Community College
maruoke@sunysuffolk.edu

Minu Mathur, 58
College of San Mateo
mathur@smccd.edu

Marcia Maurycy, 45
Sage College of Albany
maurym@sage.edu

Karla M. McLucas, 69
Bennett College for
Women
kmclucas@bennett.edu

Carl Milofsky, 50
Bucknell University
milofsky@bucknell.edu

Kenneth W. Mohney, 17
Monroe County
Community College
kmohney@monroeccc.edu

Tina Mougouris, 90
San Jacinto College—
Central
Tina.Mougouris@sjcd.edu

Lucy Ogburn, 65
Middlesex Community
College
ogburnl@middlesex.mass.
edu

Margaret Platt Jendrek, 39
Miami University
Babbie *Basics* 4e IRM/TB

Nathan W. Pino, 61, 98
Texas State University and
Robert F. Meier
University of Nebraska
Sociology of Deviant Behavior, 13E, IRMTB

Judith Pintar, 46, 56, 101
University of Illinois at
Urbana-Champaign
Brym/Lie *Sociology* 3e
IRM

Rebecca Plante, 18
Ithaca College
rplante@ithaca.edu

Dwaine Plaza, 59
Oregon State University
dplaza@orst.edu

Timothy D. Levonyan
Radloff, 19
SUNY Fredonia
levonyan@fredonia.edu

Kevin Randall, 20
Bradley University
*Lecture Ideas for Courses
on the Family*, Vol. 1, p. 74

John T. Robich, 102
Richmond Community
College
johnr@richmondcc.edu

Thomas W. Segady, 95
Stephen F. Austin State
University
tsegady@sfasu.edu

Cynthia K. Shinabarger
Reed, 91
Tarrant County College
Strong *Marriage and
Family Experience* 10e
IRM/TB

Amy Slater, 51
Mott Community College -
Blue River
amy.slater@mcckc.edu

Frances Staten, 21
Grambling State University
fstaten@bellsouth.net

Jacqueline Steingold, 21
Wayne County Community
College
steingoldj@sbcglobal.net

J. Mark Thomas, 22
Madison Area Technical
College
jmthomas@matcmadison.
edu

Vincent G. Thomas, 23,
69
Black Hawk College
vgthomas@qconline.com

Bob Transon, 66
Milwuakee Area Technical
College
transonr@matc.edu

Linda Vanella, 24
Suffolk County
Community College
lindavanella@mac.com

Shiela Venkataswamy, 71
McHenry County College
svenkata@mchenry.edu

J.B. Watson, JR., 25
Stephen F. Austin State
University
jwatson@sfasu.edu

Georgie Ann Weatherby, 52
Gonzaga University
weatherb@gonzaga.edu

Patrick Webb, 26
Lamar University
patrickwebb@hotmail.com

John R. Weeks, 99
San Diego State University
Online IMTB for Week's
Population, 10E

Michael E. Weissbuch, 95
Xavier University
weissbuc@xavier.edu

Terry Whisnant, 34
Southside Virginia
Community College
terry.whisnant@sv.vccs.edu

Frank White, 35
University of North Dakota
frank_white@und.nodak.
edu

D.R. Wilson, 35, 46, 84, 87, 91, 96, 103
Houston Baptist University
IRM for Kendall *Essentials*
and IRM for Kendall
Sociology in Our Times

Michael J. Witkowski, 47
University of Detroit
Mercy
witkowmj@udmercy.edu

Anne Wortham, 53
Rappahannock Community
College
awortham@rcc.vccs.edu

TOPIC ONE

General Teaching Tactics

Janet S. Armitage
St. Mary's University
jarmitage1@stmarytx.edu

Two interactive exercises: 1) pop music analysis and 2) paper writing workshops.

Music analysis requires students to select any mass consumed song and provide a general social meaning for the song (e.g., the lay interpretation) and then advance the interpretation through a conceptual application. Students locate "indicators" for the concept in the song's lyrics and explain each in an oral presentation.

The paper workshop uses basic sociological writing skills applied to a course topic, such as deviance or poverty. All students work in groups and develop theses, abstracts, and brief literature reviews. They receive feedback from peers as well as peer grades.

Mark Bird
College of Southern Nevada
mark.bird@ccsn.edu

This is a tactic I have successfully used for a few semesters in 101 classes. On the first day of class, I have students sign up to give a 3-10 minute intro on a text chapter. I cover the text chapters in sequence. So, as an example, when I get to chapter 7, the student who signed up for this chapter presents key info

1

relative to chapter 7. I've had students type chapter info, define key terms, outline the chapter on the board before class starts, and even put the chapter into a PowerPoint presentation. This tactic gets students more interested in the chapter and allows the instructor to expand relative to what the student presented.

Shelly Brown-Jeffy
University of North Carolina at Greensboro
slbrown2@uncg.edu

Sociology 101: Introduction to Sociology

Sociological Analysis of a Popular Movie
Due Date: Varies.
Length: 5-7 pages
Format: Double-spaced with one-inch margins and standard 12-point font.

The purpose of this assignment is for you to think sociologically about the subject matter in popular movies. During the semester we will learn about sociology and how it applies to the various aspects of the society in which we live. This exercise will allow you to integrate and reflect upon the reading and the lecture material by applying it to the context of the film.

The paper should have at least four parts. The first part should have the credits for the movie (single spaced). Then, the next parts should be the summary of the movie, the sociological significance of the movie, and a critique of the movie. Please label the parts accordingly.

The Credits
The report should begin with the type of information found in a basic movie review. Begin your report with very basic information about the film such as its credits. Please include the name of the movie, the year of release, along with names of the director, producers, and principal actors including the names of their characters in the movie. Also, indicate the film genre if applicable (e.g., comedy, documentary, drama) and whether the film is based on or adapted from a book or play, fiction or non-fiction. This section can and should be single-spaced.

The Summary
Next, briefly describe the setting (i.e., time and place the movie takes place for the story) and summarize the plot of the movie. Be as specific as possible. For example, if the setting is Los Angeles, CA, put that in the review. Remember to be brief in your retelling of the story, because you want to devote much more of your time to reporting what is sociologically important about the story. The summary should be no more than two pages.

Sociological Significance
First, relate how concepts, dynamics and issues that we have covered in class manifest in the film. When applicable, use the terms we have used in class to elaborate upon what you observed in the movie. This is very important to the paper. Strive for precision, specificity, and elaboration in this application, and discuss these concepts, dynamics and issues in the language of sociology. This is a sociological analysis. When applicable, give specific examples from the movie.

General Teaching Tactics

The Critique
Finally, offer a critique of the film according to its portrayal of the major sociological concept. Does it follow along with what we have read in class? Where does it follow along sociologically? Where does it diverge? Which sociological concept(s) is (are) most salient in the movie? Do the 'facts' of the film correspond with the research that we have reviewed in class? Identify at least one strength and one weakness of the film as a realistic portrayal of the sociological topic, as viewed through a sociological lens. In doing so, focus on assessing character presentation and imagery, and any obvious 'assumptions' or 'conclusions' you believe were made by the filmmakers. Support your points; offer supporting material. Offer a final statement indicating whether or not you would recommend this film to 1) other sociologists and 2) the general public, explaining why in both cases, and whether this is a good or bad portrayal of the sociological phenomenon.

Tawny Brown-Warren
Columbia College
tbrownwarren@cougars.ccis.edu

A strategy that I utilize to make a topic fun or interesting for students is to challenge them to find a current event that mostly resembles the topics we are discussing in class. Once identified by the student, he/she is required to write a 500-word essay on how it relates to the topic we are discussing. By relating the topics discussed to real-life events, the student is more motivated to learn and has more of a vested interested in performing to the best of his/her abilities.

Thom Curtis
University of Hawaii at Hilo
thomc@hawaii.edu

On the first day, I project two photos that will provide the focal points for our examination of sociological theories and methods throughout the semester. The first is a photo my father took at the Dachau concentration camp showing local German citizens loading bodies of dead inmates into a horse drawn cart. The second is of the explosion that followed the second plane's impact into the World Trade Center. As the class examines various facets of applied and theoretical sociology, we come back to those two photos and discuss the different ways sociologists study and explain initiation of and reaction to these significant events. Having specific subjects that can be confronted through many different lenses helps students understand the way various sociological techniques and paradigms contribute to a broader understanding of how society works. We study the photos and the events they represent through both micro and macro sociological perspectives. It is not a stretch to tie the constructs from virtually every chapter in the textbook to these two photos.

William Danaher
College of Charleston
danaherw@cofc.edu

I do group exercises that require reading beforehand or watching a film, then discussing this in small groups, and presenting results to the class. The groups remain the same throughout the semester and rotate presenters, so everyone gets to participate. My current favorite is my methods exercise,

where students must identify and discuss a number of different research methods and present their discussion and analysis to the class.
Cross-referenced with Research Methods

Robin Ersing
University of South Florida
rersing@cas.usf.edu

Role Play Re-Play: I use this technique to get students actively engaged in the course material for that lecture. I sort through the topic we are covering that day and determine if some aspect can be conveyed through role-play (e.g. social justice issues on discrimination, etc). I then create a role-play scenario that requires three phases. Each phase becomes more focused and incorporates new learning from the reading and class discussion/feedback. The first role-play is usually broad in scope with the students having to do their best to figure out how to handle a situation. We debrief as a class and I list on the board some concepts from the assigned reading on how the situation could be improved. That sets up the second role-play (or as I call it - the re-play). This demonstrates the same situation but with a bit more direction, guiding students from what they have learned. Another debriefing takes place and this time we strategize ways to further integrate the course material. That leads to the third and final role-play re-play with students acting out the same scenario with a much better outcome. The class is then able to compare/contrast the changes and discuss how each component helped or hindered the situation.

Maxine Elmont
MassBay Community College
Melmont@massbay.edu

Here is a class activity that I use after discussion of a topic in the text i.e., healthcare, family, education, etc:
-The class is divided into groups of 5-6 people.
-Each group is to decide what aspect of the topic they feel needs to be improved/changed.
-The next step is to list the changes they feel will be necessary.
-The group is then told they will have whatever resources they need to complete the changes.
-Then they have to state very specifically HOW they would implement each change to reach the desired goal(s).
-Each group is to share with the class what they have done and the reason(s) for it. Anyone in the class may ask question(s) of the group.

Maxine Elmont
MassBay Community College
MELMONT@massbay.edu

A two-part activity using the library as a resource and the class for discussion:
1. Library research
    a. Students are asked to select any topic that interests them; it must relate to sociology.
    b. Read an article from a professional journal on that topic.
    c. Write the following using no more than two 5x8 cards:
        i. article's citation
        ii. a summary of the article

iii. critique of HOW the author(s) presented the material

iv. compare the information in the article to similar material in the textbook citing the pages

2. Share and discuss the articles in class on the assigned date

   a. The class is divided into groups of 5-6 students
   b. The group selects a recorder and the members read their articles while the recorder takes notes
   c. A discussion of how the articles agree, disagree, etc. takes place after all articles have been read
   d. The recorders share their notes with the class. Anyone may ask the group a question.

3. Cards are given to the instructor to be graded.

I find the majority of the students are more open and enjoy the small group activities. True organization is the key for the large classes or bedlam reigns supreme.

Ryan G. Fletcher
Brookhaven College (DCCCD) Dallas, TX
rgfletch7

I invite students in my Intro to Sociology class to bring a video clip to class (maximum length three minutes) that relates to the current chapter we are covering. This video clip can be from a Hollywood or Independent movie, a documentary, a television series or commercial, a cartoon, or even a home video. I provide guidelines with regard to content (no curse words or sexual content beyond what is normally viewed on network television). I generally allow two or three of these quick presentations at the beginning of every class (except exam days) with the presenting student given a maximum of two minutes to explain how the video relates to what is currently under study. At the end of the week, all students turn in a secret ballot to choose which student provided the most applicable video that week and that student receives five extra-credit points on his or her next exam. The students love it and really look forward to it. It has increased student attendance and participation. It has encouraged the back of the room "corner-dwellers" to become involved with the rest of the class (some of them turn into outright hams!) Another added advantage is that students actually get to teach each other using their own popular culture format. On days when there are no student presenters, I try to have a video clip of my own to show.

Patrick E. Fontane
St. Louis College of Pharmacy
pfontane@stlcop.edu

This program requires a subscription to the daily Gallup Poll reports. The cost is approximately $100 per year. (Students like this source because they see the data before it appears in the public media.) Most topics presented are appropriate for an Introduction to Sociology class. They are short (3-4 page) survey ("public opinion") reports on current issues, usually accompanied by graphic representations of the data. It is best to use this procedure to REVIEW course content rather than when introducing relevant content. This gives students an opportunity to apply what they have learned. There should always be some students in the class who can lead in this way.

General Teaching Tactics

Highlight the report and present the graphics. Ask students to explain: 1) what the content means and, 2) the distribution of responses ("why?"). Occasionally it is necessary to discuss the method of query (questions, sample, confidence intervals, etc.). Students usually enjoy discussing the issue and learn they can apply what they know, thus increasing overall class/student participation.

EXAMPLE: Report established that high school males were decreasing their tobacco use whereas high school girls were maintaining their rate of cigarette smoking. The relevant topics are social structure(s) and socialization.

Kristie A. Ford
Skidmore College
kford@skidmore.edu

"FORCED CHOICES" EXERCISE

Objectives:
- To engage students with sociological concepts and/or theories in an interactive way
- To encourage thoughtful self-reflection and intergroup discussion
- To bring awareness to student's own preconceptions, values, and beliefs

Preparation:
Time allotment: 20 minutes (as an "icebreaker" exercise); 30-45 minutes (to allow for more in-depth discussion)

Materials needed: Large open area that permits students to move around freely; list of "forced choices" statements

"Forced Choices" Statements: These statements can vary widely depending upon the sociological concepts you are covering for that particular class period. Below are some sample statements I created to help students think more critically about various theoretical perspectives of gender:

- Men and women are fundamentally the same and should be treated exactly the same.
- It is possible to meet people and not notice and/or ascribe a gender to them.
- Boys are naturally more aggressive than girls.
- Gender difference is an outcome of gender inequality.
- Gender is a context and time dependent performance.
- Gender is largely determined by a person's physical anatomy and hormones.
- Gender is fluid and malleable.
- Children are born gender neutral and learn sex roles early in life.
- Gender is a combination of nature and nurture.
- Gender is rooted in our psyche.
- Gender is socially determined and cannot exist outside of social interaction.

Instructions:

On the left side of the black board, write "agree" and on the right side of the board, write "disagree." Ask students to stand up and push the desks to the perimeter of the room. Explain to the students that you will read a series of statements.

General Teaching Tactics

After the statement is read, students should silently move to the left side of the room if they "agree" with the statement and to the right if they "disagree." Inform them that there is no "neutral" position – in other words, they are forced to make a choice.

The instructor should read the first statement and ask the students to move to the appropriate side of the room. Pause. Ask one or two students on each side to explain why they moved to the left or the right. Allow a few minutes for discussion and then move on to the next statement. Repeat as time permits.

Debriefing Questions:
- What are your initial reactions to this activity?
- What statements were easy? More challenging? Why?
- What did you learn about yourself during this activity? What values inform your position?
- What did you learn about others? Were there any surprises?
- How does this activity connect to the readings for today? How does this activity connect to our previous conversations in this course?

NOTE: I often do this activity twice –once in the beginning of the semester and then again at the end of the semester. By the end of the semester, students should have a more nuanced understanding of the sociological concepts and theories, enabling the class to move to a deeper level of analysis and discussion.
Cross-referenced with Gender

LaKeisha Crye Green
Delgado Community College
lcrye@dcc.edu

I always have my students play a game called "Who Wants to be a Sociologist?" to review for upcoming exams. The game is similar to "Who Wants to be a Millionaire" but instead of receiving money, students are awarded bonus points on their exam if they answer their question correctly. Each student has the opportunity to participate once for a possible total of two points to be added to their exam grade. Students can use one out of two life lines if they do not know the answer to their question. They can either "ask a classmate" or ask the instructor to "take away two of the wrong answers." By using the life lines, everyone is practically a winner! I believe that this game is a great way for students to learn and to test themselves by using the sample test questions that are generated for the game. This game is also a great way for students to learn a little bit about one another. I always have the students come to the front of the class and introduce themselves. Students love it!

Hui M Huo
Highline Community College
hhuo@highline.edu

The use of analogies to illustrate and explain hard to grasp concepts.

Example: Eggs hatch only at a certain temperature, where temperature can be understood as the outside condition that an entity must meet in order to materialize. In this case, it could be thought of as a "social structure which constrains or causes an act to happen." Only eggs do not react or initiate as humans. The same analogy applies to the question of variation among humans. Rock does not hatch at the same temperature because it is an entirely different category. Brown eggs or white eggs possess essentially the same quality as diversity among humans.

Aiden Kenny
County College of Morris
ajk33@ptonline.net

My classes usually have about 35 students. In order to get individual participation I have found the "fishbowl" to be an effective tool. Readings or issues are assigned for the next class. When the class meets, five or six students are asked to join me in the "fishbowl" in the center of the class. The current topic is discussed in detail. Anyone listening in may join by switching with a participant. I believe it accomplishes a couple of things:

- Students must introduce each other.
- The topic is able to be investigated from a number of perspectives.
- Lastly, students are not aware who will be called on to sit in the "fishbowl" until it is convened.

Grace Keyes
St. Mary's University
gkeyes@stmarytx.edu

Teaching Sociology with News Events
"News of the Week Assignments"

OBJECTIVE: To encourage students to keep up with the news (local, national, world) and to apply sociological concepts and insights to such events. The assignment encourages the application of the "sociological perspective" and specific concepts and theories as they are being learned.

INSTRUCTIONS: Students are asked to find a news story in the local paper, a national news magazine or newspaper such as the *New York Times*. News stories reported on television or posted on the Internet are also acceptable. Even stories about celebrities, contemporary music, sports, or items students are interested in can be useful, although I encourage more significant 'newsworthy' items.

The student then writes a very brief paper on the story with the two following requirements: (a) a succinct synopsis of main elements of the story, (b) a discussion of the news item using sociological concepts at hand. For example, if the class is learning about the distinction between "issues" and "troubles" as discussed by C. Wright Mills in his "sociological imagination," then the student could illustrate or discuss how these concepts are illustrated in the story or what insights the concepts bring to the story. Or if the topic is "deviance" then the student might apply a specific theory such as the 'differential association theory' or other relevant concepts to the story. Students are asked to try to select stories that are most relevant for the concepts being covered each week. The students come prepared with their written paper on a given day of the week to also discuss their 'news item' in class.

VARIATIONS: (a) The assignment also works well if the instructor selects and assigns a specific news story for the class to read as a whole. (b) Students may be asked to complete the

assignment individually or in small groups of two to four students. (c) Rather than a written paper, the student may simply be asked to come to class ready to discuss and analyze the news story (whether selected by instructor or student). (d) A weekly report may be required of all students or alternately, each student or group of students may be given a specific date on which their report is due, thus reducing the number of reports the instructor has to read but ensuring that each week at least one news story is discussed.
Cross-referenced with Sociological Perspectives

Gary R. Lemons
Scottsdale Community College
gary.lemons@sccmail.maricopa.edu

My goal is to get the students to come to class prepared and to create opportunities for each student to have something to say in class. My classes have around 30 students. I have written 10 to 20 homework questions for each of the 16 chapters I use from Stark's *Sociology*. As a homework assignment, the students write answers to each of the questions, bring two copies to class (I keep one) and we go over the questions and answers in class. I call on students by name and they answer the questions orally in class. We then discuss the meaning and context of the answers and I integrate what they say into my response, which in some cases becomes a mini-lecture, but always provides a way to provide students with something to say in class. Often the students orally add to each other's answers. It keeps the students involved and on their toes, as they can be called upon at any time. They get credit for the homework and they can use the homework assignment as a study guide for the exam. The homework questions seem to relieve some of the anxiety that students have, and I can now count on discussion and my tests are more challenging than before. I've been doing this for about five years and it works beautifully. I grade the homework on completeness, but not content. I find that the exams I now give are at a higher level than before, and the class is much more interactive. The students get credit for studying and taking notes from the text and then they come to class prepared for the day's lesson. They always know what will be covered in class and what will be on the tests. I create the questions by looking at the multiple choice test bank. You can see the homework questions on my course website: http://www.scottsdalecc.edu/lemons/soc101/index.html.

Kenneth W. Mohney
Monroe County Community College
kmohney@monroeccc.edu

As part of all introductory classes at my college, students are required to write a term paper that details some type of research on a particular topic. Over the last several years I have read hundreds of papers on divorce, marriage, effects of TV, etc, etc. With so many being the same or very similar in content I decided to do something a little different that could also be used as a classroom teaching aid. As an alternative to a traditional term paper (focusing primarily on literature research) I have allowed students to design and implement survey research on a topic that interests them. This can be either used as a team or individual project. I ask them to define a problem or come up with a hypothesis on a topic (for instance, one that involves student problems with the campus), formulate a sampling design and a questionnaire, then have the students collect their data. Once collected, they are to analyze the problem using the data and come up with a conclusion. All is then written up in a paper. By using this as an option, rather than the traditional term paper, students gain practical experience in working together, using real research techniques (leading to a better overall understanding of the material) and report more satisfaction in the project. The project can then be used as a basis for classroom presentation, leading to additional learning opportunities. Each team that conducts a survey can present the methods and results of the survey to the class. The other students can then evaluate the survey in terms of all of the things we have discussed previously regarding proper research techniques. They can gauge whether the sample size and techniques used could adequately address the question and other issues. In using this technique, I seem to have greater student interest and deeper involvement. The greatest benefit is, however, that students better learn the material since I believe that few things aid learning better than practical hands on work.

Rebecca Plante
Ithaca College
rplante@ithaca.edu

On the first day of class, I know that I will be confronting students' assumption that sociology is just common sense. To begin to disrupt this common and wrong assumption, I give a first day of class quiz - about 8-10 questions, multiple choice. Topics touch on major social institutions and things that students tend to simply assume, without reference to data. It helps students start chatting with the person next to them, especially if I ask them to discuss their answers before committing. In a huge class, a professor could require students to work in groups to determine answers. When I give the answers, it provides a way to immediately get students participating. I can ask what their logic was, their thought process, etc. This sets a good model for my course: I expect participation and I encourage it, and I expect critical thinking (and will teach students how to do this). It also enables me to start talking about the use of data, statistics, and the like. So this seemingly simple quiz starts the class on a good foot and communicates a lot - overtly and covertly - about what the course will be like for the rest of the term.

Timothy D. Levonyan Radloff
SUNY Fredonia
levonyan@fredonia.edu

Throughout the sixteen week semester, students are asked to bring in what I refer to as a "music selection" that relates to any of the topics (e.g., religion, family, suicide, stratification, race and gender inequality, sexuality, identity, poverty, war etc.) we address in class. A music selection can be a music video or song from any genre of music—e.g., Buddhist music, rhapsody, rock, metal, hip-hop, opera, or country.

Each student who brings in a music selection introduces herself or himself and explains how her or his particular music selection relates to the class readings and lectures. Then, after proper introduction, the music selection is played. The purpose in doing this musical activity is not only to evoke emotions such as excitement and perseverance (as we all know music can do), but also to encourage them to use their sociological imagination. What I mean by using their sociological imagination is to see how their own individual lives are shaped by social forces such as the media, law and politics, economy, religion, education etc. that exist outside themselves.

Furthermore, in addition to encouraging reflection on the lyrics, I believe that listening to as many diverse perspectives as possible about the issues covered in class, especially through the arts, can have a profound effect on student learning. Ever since I've been doing this, I noticed that class discussions have been livelier and involve more students. In addition, for their final projects, students are asked to write a theory paper that requires them to apply one of the three major sociological perspectives on social order (i.e., symbolic interactionism, structural functionalist, and conflict) to a book, art, or a song. I've noticed that a good portion of students are very enthusiastic about applying sociological theory to a song that has deeply affected them.

Kevin Randall
Bradley University
Lecture Ideas for Courses on the Family, **Vol. 1, p. 74**
In order to encourage (a) student preparation before class, and (b) completion of the assigned reading, I randomly assign two to three students the responsibility to prepare a skit or innovative methodology of their own choosing for that particular class topic. The students enjoy having fun in the classroom and do a good job of engaging their peers in the topic. I find the class is ready for involvement when I begin. This simple activity, which can be used in grading, is applicable to any discipline and class setting (face to face or distance).

Frances Staten
Grambling State University
fstaten@bellsouth.net

Teaching Theory and Research in the Cemetery: a Field Trip

Example: Students are required to use the monuments or tombstones in the cemetery to obtain social/demographic information (year and date of birth and death, age, gender, and marital family status (husband/wife/children)) about persons buried in one of the oldest African American Cemeteries in Grambling, Louisiana. Cultural/Social Symbols are also identified--like praying hand, angel and various emblems affiliated with a given organization, i.e. Masonic Lodge. The main theoretical questions: What is the function of the cemetery? What are the different type of symbols in the cemetery?

Jacqueline Steingold
Wayne County Community College
steingoldj@sbcglobal.net

Introductory exercise is critical to creating a team and open environment for sharing and interaction. I distribute the following "Get Acquainted Interview" and pair students up (if there's not an even number I participate).

1. What is your name?
2. Where are you from?
3. What are some of the things you like to do?
4. Tell me one thing about yourself that surprises people.
5. What job would you least like to have?
6. What job would you most like to have?

7. What is your career goal?
8. If you won $100,000 how would you spend it?
9. Tell me one good thing that has happened in your life.

Laughs result, interesting and unexpected responses, great ice breaker.

J. Mark Thomas
Madison Area Technical College
jmthomas@matcmadison.edu

An introduction to sociology seems to me a topical class, letting the beginning student know the kinds of inquiries distinct to sociology. The problem is how to do more than rote teaching and learning, especially from the "phone book" style introduction books widely in use. With the larger texts, one can pick and choose, of course, but only by simultaneously losing some topical material. I am convinced that students become adult learners only when they become deeply immersed in the questions to which sociological inquiry is an answer.

Thus, I have my students come prepared for class with written efforts to state both what is the explicit or implicit question in the reading and the author's fundamental answer. That puts students in dialogue with thinkers, rather than leaving them asking what I want them to memorize.

I also want introduction students to get a glimpse of how classics in the field have constructed the questions to be addressed and the methods they bring to their answers. Thus, I pick a reader with selections that do this, and I have them read in correspondence with the questions being asked in the basic text.

Finally, I emphasize that all data in books is potentially out of date by the time it is put into print. Hence, I use a computer program that addresses introductory topics by linking students to relevant websites (at least as some editor sees relevance). Together, this provides me with a narrative text organized around the philosophical questions implicit in sociological inquiry, a reader with snippets of topical essays from classics in the field, and a computer-aided inquiry that provides contemporary information.

Vincent G. Thomas
Black Hawk College
vgthomas@qconline.com

In my first introductory class I write my name and ask a question. "What kind of Indian am I?" I am originally from India. I am dark skinned and balding. I wear a cap that says "Native American" or another which is obviously Native American designed with bead work and a white bison. I wear a bolo tie which has an arrowhead on it. I ask the students to write their first impressions of me and try to answer the question. After I collect the 2X5 cards I had distributed for answers, I explain some (very few) of the students correctly identify me with India (generally they are students who are nurses or those who have had contact with Asian Indian doctors). Most of the students are unsure of my true background. I begin to explain how we learn to form impressions of others, based on names (Thomas is a familiar South-Indian Christian name) the Vincent comes from my mother's side of the family (she was from Goa--Catholics.) So even though my name is very American, it was created in India.

General Teaching Tactics

I belong to a Native American coalition here and have received my adornments as gifts. So this is an icebreaker for me, because now I ask the students to write their backgrounds on another set of 2x5 cards for me. Then I ask them to pair off and talk about themselves briefly to one another. Some of the information they have given me about themselves I share at the second class. Such as how many nurses, veterans, where they came from originally, etc. and what the goals of the students are without revealing personal information they may have written about themselves. We all learn from this experience that we are an interconnected society with many common goals, even though some live in the cities and some are from rural towns. This experience also is a new experience in communicating with people with whom they may never have had the opportunity to do so before and to learn about their cultural backgrounds. Of course, all this does not happen instantaneously in the first class. But the communication and learning from one another continues throughout the course. We relate our interconnectedness to current events.
Cross-referenced with Race and Ethnicity

Linda Vanella
Suffolk County community college
lindavanella@mac.com

I ask the students to dance to a subject, yes dance. They are forced to use some boday movement to a 'subject matter they thought belonged in a 'book''. They always respond positively and share in writing how impressed they are with such an assignment.

J.B. Watson, Jr.
Stephen F. Austin State University
jwatson@sfasu.edu

Service-learning: Students complete a minimum four hours of volunteer work in a five-week summer session, or eight hours in a regular semester in a community setting. Students keep a log of their daily experiences, and write three reflection papers of 250-500 words each.

The first paper is an overview of the community setting where they are volunteering, and a discussion of any preconceived notions they may hold about the service-learning experience.

The second paper is a mid-point reflection of what they feel they are learning and an application of two or more sociological concepts, theories, or methods that enhance their understanding of the community population served by their agency.

The third paper is a closure reflection paper applying two or more additional sociological concepts, and detailing their overall experience in the service-learning project.

The second and third reflection papers are due as drafts on class dates approximately one-third and two-thirds of the way through the semester when the class engages in group reflection (class discussion) on their experiences. The student log and three reflection papers are turned in as a Service-Learning Portfolio near the end of the semester.

General Teaching Tactics

Patrick Webb
Lamar University
patrickwebb@hotmail.com

With regards to establishing and developing critical thought among students, I suggest the following classroom teaching measures: 1) student debates/discussions, 2) student role playing activities, and 3) daily journal entries.

1. When utilizing methods that establish and develop debate/discussion skills among students, I suggest having the students engage in a classroom debate or discussion regarding a controversial topic that stems from an assigned chapter reading as stated according to the syllabus. This exercise will attempt to ensure that students are: a) reading their assigned chapters and b) stimulate discussion regarding various relative aspects associated with the content of the assigned chapter reading. Such measures have proven to be advantageous in terms of student-instructor interaction prior to the lecturing period.

2. Student role-playing activities allow students to identify with the practical aspects associated with seemingly difficult theoretical concepts and paradigms. Thes activities also afford students the opportunity to express themselves in an honest and creative manner. Like debates/discussions, these activities should be used in an attempt to stimulate ideas and interest prior to the lecturing period.

3. Daily journal entries are utilized to establish and develop creative writing skills. From a critical standpoint, students are advised and challenged to present opposing arguments in relation to topics presented by the instructor. This method, like the aforementioned measures, is designed to help students to express themselves in a creative and professional manner.

TOPIC TWO

Sociological Perspectives

Jan AbuShakrah
Portland Community College
Andersen/Taylor Ess.4e IRM, p. 7

Theoretical Perspectives.

To insure that students understand the major sociological perspectives, present them with an issue of contemporary concern - like homelessness - and have them describe how they think functionalists, conflict theorists, and symbolic interactionists would approach the issue. This could be conducted as an in-class exercise or assigned as a take-home paper and discussed later. This activity could also be an online discussion in WebTutor™. In addition to exploring the approaches of the major theoretical perspectives, this exercise could also be organized by social location. Groups of students could be assigned to represent diverse social classes, race/ethnicity, and gender perspectives.

Jill Harrison
Rhode Island College
jharrison@ric.edu

I ask students to pick three "Top Ten" songs off any billboard/chart and analyze their content for sociological concepts. We develop the hypotheses to test in class, so the class tests all the same items.

Sociological Perspectives

For example, in an introductory sociology class, we can use the themes of race, class, and gender to analyze the content and link them with C. Wright Mills, Marx, etc. Hypotheses are student generated, so they will vary. For example, to test a Marxian concept about inequality, one hypothesis might be, "Women are more likely to be victimized in song lyrics than are men." "Victimization" is carefully defined in class.

This initial hypothesis can also be expanded to include dimensions of race and class. Students are taught to code the data and create a table. Then they must write a paper that addresses the theory, the data, their analysis, and conclusions. It's a good length for introductory students and gets them using material they are comfortable with while covering all the bases: scientific method, qualitative data analysis, theory, and application of theory, and an original analysis. Students seem to enjoy it!
Cross-referenced with Research Methods

Erik Fritsvold
University of San Diego
erikf@sandiego.edu

Character Participation: Throughout the semester, each student will give a two-minute presentation on an important figure in the broad field of sociology. Each presentation will begin by introducing your character in the first person ("Hi, I am Emile Durkheim"), followed by a summary of their major contributions to sociology and/or a description of how their life story connects to themes from the course.

Presentations begin on the second class meeting, thus every student should be prepared to present beginning our third class meeting. It will not be revealed when each individual presentation will take place; "characters" will be called (sometimes more than once) throughout each lecture throughout the entire course. So, students should be prepared to give their presentation, beginning next class, and at each and every class meeting for the rest of the semester at a moment's notice. There are no make-up opportunities; if you do not attend, or are unprepared to present the day your character is called, you earn a zero on this assignment and lose a significant percentage of your final grade.

I will randomly assign each enrolled student to a "character." For some characters, additional information is provided to help guide the substance of the presentation. Presentations will be graded on content, organization and clarity. These presentations will help introduce new figures and topics to the course, give students another mechanism to contribute to the class holistically and be a relatively lively and fun way to earn a portion of one's course grade.

The above exercise has proven to be engaging, fun and substantively valuable. It also serves as a de facto attendance policy. It allows each student to serve as a 'resident expert' on that particular figure in sociology. This exercise does pose an organizational challenge. By assigning characters at the beginning of the course, you commit to covering certain materials.

Sociological Perspectives

Grace Keyes
St. Mary's University
gkeyes@stmarytx.edu

Teaching Sociology with News Events
"News of the Week Assignments"

OBJECTIVE: To encourage students to keep up with the news (local, national, world) and to apply sociological concepts and insights to such events. The assignment encourages the application of the "sociological perspective" and specific concepts and theories as they are being learned.

INSTRUCTIONS: Students are asked to find a news story in the local paper, a national news magazine, or a newspaper such as the *New York Times*. News stories reported on television or posted on the Internet are also acceptable. Even stories about celebrities, contemporary music, sports, or items students are interested in can be useful, although I encourage more significant 'newsworthy' items.

The student then writes a very brief paper on the story with the two following requirements: (a) a succinct synopsis of main elements of the story, (b) a discussion of the news item using sociological concepts at hand.

For example, if the class is learning about the distinction between "issues" and "troubles" as discussed by C. Wright Mills in his "sociological imagination," then the student could illustrate or discuss how these concepts are illustrated in the story or what insights the concepts bring to the story. Or if the topic is "deviance" then the student might apply a specific theory such as the 'differential association theory' or other relevant concepts to the story. Students are asked to try to select stories that are most relevant for the concepts being covered each week. The students come prepared with their written paper on a given day of the week to also discuss their 'news item' in class.

VARIATIONS: (a) The assignment also works well if the instructor selects and assigns a specific news story for the class to read as a whole. (b) Students may be asked to complete the assignment individually or in small groups of two to four students. (c) Rather than a written paper, the student may simply be asked to come to class ready to discuss and analyze the news story (whether selected by instructor or student). (d) A weekly report may be required of all students or alternately, each student or group of students may be given a specific date on which their report is due, thus reducing the number of reports the instructor has to read but ensuring that each week at least one news story is discussed.
Cross-referenced with General Teaching Tactics

Etsuko Maruoka
Suffolk Country Community College
maruoke@sunysuffolk.edu

The purposes of this exercise are: 1) to increase students' understanding of gender socialization; 2) to learn the basic research methods in sociology; and 3)to apply the three basic sociological perspectives in real life settings.

First, I give my students the following assignment. In the following class I make them compare their findings and analysis. At the last half of the class time period, I facilitate a discussion on the three points described above.

Sociological Perspectives

Assignment:

"One must learn by doing the thing, for though you think you know it - you have no certainty until you try." - Sophocles (BC 495-406)

Do one of the following two exercises.

OPTION 1:
1. Go to a toy store in your local area. By using the technique of Observational Research, observe and describe how the boys' and girls' sections are different by focusing on the following criteria:

       a. What kinds of things are displayed and sold in each section?

       b. What kinds of words or phrases are used to describe the toys in each section?

       c. What colors and decorations are used in each section?

       d. What sounds do those toys make?

       e. Where are those toys meant to be played with?

2. Based on your field notes, analyze and discuss why you think there are differences by using one of the following sociological perspectives introduced in class and textbook – i.e. Structural-Functionalism, Conflict Theory, and Symbolic Interactionism.

OPTION 2:

1. Select a film that is produced for children from the list below. By using the technique of Content Analysis, describe it by focusing on the following criteria:

       a. Who are the characters and what are their demographic characteristics – i.e. gender, age, class, etc.?

b. What themes about gender does it include?

c. How does the film convey dominant societal values and norms based on gender? What are they?

d. How do the visual images, such as the characters' physical figure, kinds of clothes and colors that they put on, and gestures that they use, support the gender norms and values?

2. Analyze and discuss what lesson boys and girls who watch the film learn by using one of the following sociological perspectives introduced in class and textbook – i.e. Structural-Functionalism, Conflict Theory, and Symbolic Interactionism.

Film List - Aladdin - Batman - Beauty and the Beast - Cinderella - Hercules - Snow White and the Seven Dwarfs - Spiderman - Superman - The Little Mermaid - The Sword in the Stone - The Lion King - Tarzan
Cross-referenced with Gender and Research Methods

Etsuko Maruoka
Suffolk Country Community College
maruoke@sunysuffolk.edu

In order to increase students' understanding of the concept of "Sociological Imagination," I give my students the following assignment: Students give a short presentation to their group members during the following class and discuss how their individual life is connected to the larger structure of the society that they belong to.

Assignment: Interview a parent or grandparent who is of the same gender as you about how they spent their spare time and what was considered to be "cool" when they were your age or a teenager. Compare them to how you and your friends enjoy your spare time. Write your reactions to your interviews by discussing why you think there are differences between you and your (grand)parent's generations by using sociological imagination*.

* "using sociological imagination" means that you have to include a discussion on what kind of social change might influence the ways in which young people enjoy their lives in different time periods.

Terry Whisnant
Southside Virginia Community College
terry.whisnant@sv.vccs.edu

During the first week of classes, students are arranged into collaborative groups to respond to a matching test. Each group's task is to match the photo of a famous sociologist with a list of sociological theories or concepts. For example, Sumner's photo should be matched with ethnocentrism; Comte with "sociologie"; Spencer with Social Darwinism. Photos are then projected onto an overhead screen and each group receives points for correct matches -- and bonuses for additional information such as nationality or primary place of study. Earned group points are distributed via consensus within the group, and later may be traded for hints on up-coming test questions.

Frank White
University of North Dakota
frank_white@und.nodak.edu

I have developed a series of Defining Features Matrices adopted from Angelo and Cross (1991) classroom assessment techniques. These three matrices are able to assess whether or not the introductory student can differentiate between the three major paradigms (Functionalist, Conflict, and Interactionism) as well as distinguish between a criticism and an assumption of each theory. It is easy-to-administer in both large lecture and lab sections, quickly graded, and provides both the instructor (or teaching assistant) and student with rapid feedback on what needs to be addressed.

D.R. Wilson
Houston Baptist University
Kendall's Ess. 5e IRM, p. 17

Theoretical Thinking: Introduce theoretical thinking by asking your students to come up with some of their own theories about "why things are the way they are." You will need to help them to refine their thinking--a great way to introduce some of the key ideas of the thinkers in this chapter. Keep asking the question "why?" to their theoretical explanations. This will help push students into more general and abstract thinking.

TOPIC THREE

Research Methods

William Danaher
College of Charleston
danaherw@cofc.edu

I do group exercises that require reading beforehand or watching a film, then discussing this in small groups, and presenting results to the class. The groups remain the same throughout the semester and rotate presenters, so everyone gets to participate. My current favorite is my methods exercise, where students must identify and discuss a number of different research methods and present their discussion and analysis to the class.
Cross-referenced with General Teaching Tactics

Jill Harrison
Rhode Island College
jharrison@ric.edu

I ask students to pick three "Top Ten" songs off any billboard/chart and analyze their content for sociological concepts. We develop the hypotheses to test in class, so the class tests all the same items. For example, in an introductory sociology class, we can use the themes of race, class, and gender to analyze the content and link them with C. Wright Mills, Marx, etc. Hypotheses are student generated, so they will vary. For example, to test a Marxian concept about inequality, one hypothesis might be, "Women are more likely

to be victimized in song lyrics than are men." "Victimization" is carefully defined in class. This initial hypothesis can also be expanded to include dimensions of race and class. Students are taught to code the data and create a table. Then they must write a paper that addresses the theory, the data, their analysis, and conclusions. It's a good length for introductory students and gets them using material they are comfortable with while covering all the bases: scientific method, qualitative data analysis, theory, and application of theory, and an original analysis. Students seem to enjoy it!
Cross-referenced with Race and Sociological Perspectives.

Diane C. Keithly
Southern University
Dckeithly@AOL.com

Today any educated person must understand how research is conducted in order to become an informed and critical consumer of information. Using Henry Tischler's text, *Introduction to Sociology*, my introduction to sociology students learn about the method and design of social research.

I introduce this chapter to the students as the most important one for their future use because we are living in an age of information. Press releases from sources such as the *New England Journal of Medicine* appearing in the local daily newspaper are often good examples of how we are constantly bombarded with new information which we can apply in our daily lives. For example, we all want to know what factors are affecting our well-being; we want to know how diet and exercise affect health and longevity. Studies using census data and social surveys also frequently appear in the media. We want to understand how rates of marriage and divorce are changing, how high school dropout rates affect society and our local community compares with others in terms of health, education and quality of life.

Students study a number of research designs: the experimental design, the social survey, participant observation, content analysis, and secondary analysis. Each design is described in the textbook and in my lectures. Students also learn about flaws in research such as poor sample design and bias in research. Students are asked to find current examples of research. A good source for my students is the local daily newspaper which is distributed free on our campus. Other instructors might want to direct their students to reputable news sources online or to the college's reading room for current periodicals. Academic sociology journals, such as the *Journal of Marriage and the Family*, also contain topics of interest to students.

Each student presents an example of a research study to the class. The student and class decide the type of research design used. Class discussion also considers critical questions about the design and the findings. The students look for shortcomings in the design of the research; this includes possible shortcomings such as researcher bias and sampling error. In this manner students learn to critically analyze information rather than passively accept everything as it is presented in the media and elsewhere.

Margaret Platt Jendrek
Miami University
Babbie Basics 4e IRM/TB, p. 221

Ask students to select an article that interests them and to analyze that report by commenting on its: 1) theoretical underpinnings, 2) methodology, 3) research design, 4) data collection technique, and 5) analyses.

Maxwell N. Kwenda
Cameron University
mkwenda@cameron.edu

I collect attendance data. I use this information to stress how attendance is positively correlated to performance in the class. By mid-semester we would have covered the research methods of the class. This would also show the students how the research process works. We can then revisit the topic by looking at the advantages and disadvantages of such a technique. This tool allows me to kill two birds with one stone.

Etsuko Maruoka
Suffolk Country Community College
maruoke@sunysuffolk.edu

The purposes of this exercise are: 1) to increase students' understanding of gender socialization; 2) to learn the basic research methods in sociology; and 3) to apply the three basic sociological perspectives in real life settings.

Research Methods

First, I give my students the following assignment. In the following class I make them compare their findings and analysis. At the last half of the class time period, I facilitate a discussion on the three points described above.

Assignment: "One must learn by doing the thing, for though you think you know it - you have no certainty until you try." - Sophocles (BC 495-406)   Do one of the following two exercises.

OPTION 1:
1. Go to a toy store in your local area. By using the technique of Observational Research, observe and describe how the boys' and girls' sections are different by focusing on the following criteria:
    a. What kinds of things are displayed and sold in each section?
    b. What kinds of words or phrases are used to describe the toys in each section?
    c. What colors and decorations are used in each section?
    d. What sounds do those toys make?
    e. Where are those toys meant to be played with?
2. Based on your field notes, analyze and discuss why you think there are differences by using one of the following sociological perspectives introduced in class and textbook – i.e. Structural-Functionalism, Conflict Theory, and Symbolic Interactionism.

OPTION 2:

1. Select a film that is produced for children from the list on the back side. By using the technique of Content Analysis, describe it by focusing on the following criteria:

    a. Who are the characters and what are their demographic characteristics – i.e. gender, age, class, etc.?

    b. What themes about gender does it include?

    c. How does the film convey dominant societal values and norms based on gender? What are they?

    d. How do the visual images, such as the characters' physical figure, kinds of clothes and colors that they put on, and gestures that they use, support the gender norms and values?

2. Analyze and discuss what lesson boys and girls who watch the film learn by using one of the following sociological perspectives introduced in class and textbook – i.e. Structural-Functionalism, Conflict Theory, and Symbolic Interactionism.

Film List - Aladdin - Batman - Beauty and Beast - Cinderella - Hercules - Snow White and the Seven Dwarfs - Spiderman - Superman - The Little Mermaid - The Sword in the Stone - The Lion King - Tarzan
Cross-referenced with Gender and Sociological Perspectives

TOPIC FOUR

Culture

Michael K. Abel
Brigham Young University-Idaho
abelm@byui.edu

I cannot remember where this idea originally came from; I don't think I came up with it, but it is a very useful and simple illustration. When I talk about globalization or taking a global perspective in my introductory sociology class I like to illustrate how everyone in the world is interconnected by having everyone look at his or her neighbor's clothing tag to find out where his or her neighbor's clothes were made. After they have had a chance to look, I have them call out the different countries that they read on the tags and I list them on the board. In a class of 40 there are usually at least 20-30 countries listed. Then we have a discussion about how what some worker is doing in China, or wherever, has made it possible for them to dress the way they do. This usually easily develops into a detailed discussion about how we live in a global society where each of us is interconnected in ways that we can hardly comprehend. We discuss many of these different connections as students come up with them. They seem to gain a greater appreciation for how their way of life is contingent upon the lives of others that they will never meet.

Carolyn Irwin Burns
Calhoun at Huntsville
irwin40328@aol.com

Hands on based on experience. A lot of my students have come from other countries. To teach cultural diversity, everyone brings a dish from his or her country, the recipe for everyone, and they dress the part if possible and tell as much about that particular culture as possible: government, religious beliefs, education, leisure activities, language, etc. Everyone learns something from everyone and they learn to appreciate each others' diverse beliefs, needs, desires and experiences.

Janet Cosbey
Eastern Illinois University
jrcosbey@eiu.edu

I was so moved by seeing the film *Crash*, which won the Oscar for Best Picture in 2005, that I decided upon leaving the theater that I would use that movie in some way in my Introduction to Sociology class. The film, directed by Canadian film director, Paul Haggis, is literally and figuratively a film about a crash that takes place on Mulholland Drive in Los Angeles, the line between the dangerous city and the posh valley. The movie is about the collision of cars, but it is also about the collision of cultures, races, and social clashes that is so prevalent in L.A. and other urban areas of our country. When the film was released on DVD I used it rather than the film I previously used, *When Cultures Collide*, to introduce the topic of culture. The students were mesmerized watching the film and this shared communal experience set the tone for the rest of the class. The discussion after the film was animated and started with the simple question "what do you think this movie is about?" It soon became clear that the students saw this more as a film about "race" than a film about "culture." However, throughout the semester students expressed heightened awareness of the impact of "culture" on social behavior and social interaction. Several assignments and test questions were based on the viewing of the film *Crash* and the movie was referred to by both students and the instructor when discussion throughout the semester focused on race and ethnicity, gender, crime, social class and power.

Tracy L. Dietz
University of Central Florida
IRMTB for Brinkerhoff's Ess. of Sociology 7E, p. 41

Guest Speakers

If you live in an area that is rich in cultural diversity, invite members from various religious and/or ethnic community organizations to speak to your class. Your campus multicultural affairs or international affairs office may be able to help you come up with potential speakers. Students gain a much greater understanding of cultural differences and similarities when they are allowed to visit with someone from a different culture. If you want to be sure the discussion ties directly into your course, you can ask the speaker(s) to address a specific topic that will be covered in a later chapter. If you want to give your class a sense of how their peers from different cultures/races/ethnicities experience life, invite a panel of minority and/or exchange students from your campus to address the class. A panel of similar-aged students can be a wonderful lesson in how popular activities such as dating vary between cultures.

Joan Ferrante
Northern Kentucky University
Ferrante 7e IRM, p. TBD

Ask students if they can think of an example of material culture in the U.S. (one that reflects the importance of the group). Hint: Public transportation and highway lanes dedicated to those who carpool are two examples. Students will find that material culture in the U.S. tends to emphasize the importance of the individual over the group.

Marcia Maurycy
Sage College of Albany
maurym@sage.edu

To begin the unit on Culture I use the first 15 minutes of the movie *The Gods Must Be Crazy*. This section clearly shows the impact that an artifact (the Coca Cola bottle) can have on a culture. Lively discussion follows the presentation.

TOPIC FIVE

Socialization

Judith Pintar
University of Illinois at Urbana-Champaign
Brym/Lie 3e IRM, p. 52-53

Ask two of your friends how they were disciplined by their parents when they were growing up. Compare and contrast the differences in discipline methods. Have your friends also tell you a little about themselves. Do you think that different discipline methods have an outcome on how an individual turns out? Discuss your findings in a short paper.

D.R. Wilson
Houston Baptist University
IRM for Kendall's Ess, 5E, p. 57

The Media as an Agent of Socialization

Take a look at the television commercials that are played during different time periods when different social groups are watching the tube:

1) During the hours when kids come home from school;
2) During Monday Night Football;
3) The middle of the day;
4) Late night.

How do these commercials contribute to racial socialization, gender socialization, and anticipatory socialization?

Michael J. Witkowski
University of Detroit Mercy
witkowmj@udmercy.edu

When discussing "street socialization" (which is often a new concept for many suburban or rural students) I ask them to identify where the following phrase or quotes come from: "The world is yours." "Every day above ground is a good day." "Say hello to my little fiend."

Invariably, almost all know these are from the Al Pacino film *Scarface*. Many students own the film or wear shirts depicting the star character. When I have their input and attention, I use it to define sociological terms like "street socialization" or "street masculinity."

Students often know many phrases from this film. I ask them to share the lessons they learned and typically get back such items as: "Don't get high on your own supply" and statements on respect and power. Then I get them to share (and at the same time hopefully see) how tragic Tony Montana is as a role model. How he is sociopathic, paranoid, misogynistic, etc. It has always stimulated great class discussion - and is known across all socio-economic groups.

Showing small clips from the film can help stimulate discussion. There are several that serve to define sociological terms...I leave it to you to find your own segment!

TOPIC SIX

Social Structure and Interaction

Jan Abu-Shakrah
Portland Community College
Andersen/Taylor 4e IRM, p. 54

Simulation.

The University of California, Santa Barbara's Case Method Website provides good materials for students to participate in simulations of societies or communities on particular issues. It includes materials on how to teach with the method, how to prepare students for role-playing, and so on. See: http://www.soc.ucsb.edu/projects/casemethod/.

Phil Gillette
University of Maryland University College - Europe
pgillette@faculty.ed.umuc.edu

I have gathered a large selection of gestures and, using the classification of beckoning, farewells, insults, and greetings, conducted a session where students (having been given the information, origin, and explanation for each gesture) act out the gesture, while explaining it.

Jeanne Humble
Bluegrass Community and Technical College
jshumb1@uky.edu

Based on the supplementary book *Global Sociology - Introducing Five Contemporary Societies* by Linda Schneider and Arnold Silverman, I divide students into different countries (e.g., Japan, Mexico or Egypt) and have students select a social institution (e.g., family, economy, political institution, religion, education or health care) and look at the following topics that should be applied to the student's particular social institution: social inequality and the distribution of wealth, culture and values, the roles of men and women, socialization, social change and deviance.

Half of the grade is a peer review from other students and half is from the professor. Students can show items from the culture, pictures, decide if they want to do individual or group posters, etc. I cover the chapters on Germany and Namibia (the !Kung). This helps to understand a more global perspective on topics that are covered in a typical sociology textbook. Sometimes students bring food from the culture.

Carol LaLiberte
Asnuntuck Community College
clalib0254@aol.com

Students in my Intro classes have to work in teams to create an ideal society and they have to present their society in a fun, creative manner at the end of the semester. I outline the requirements that they must address.

For instance, they must create a way to educate members, decide on religion(s), create a form of government and industry. I take the requirements from our intro text so that students are basically incorporating everything they have learned into their presentations. They grapple throughout with the question, "what is ideal?"

Social Structure and Interaction

As part of the presentation they are also required to create or use a song that will be their society's national anthem. At the end of each presentation, all students in the class participate in singing this national anthem that signifies their society's beliefs or values. Students grade presenters using an objective rating scale that I give them.

This culminating activity has proven worthwhile because it is a fun way to summarize all that they have learned throughout the semester, one that involves everyone. It is not, however, easy. Conflicts arise, levels of participation are not always equal and one person's notion of ideal is not another's. That is where the real learning takes place. Just like in life, disagreements must be dealt with either through the removal of students who are not doing the work (I build in mechanisms for this) and in a way that members can come together by the end of the semester. A lot is learned by this process and I refine it and change it a bit every time I do it. But in the end, students report that they learned a lot about the topics in sociology as well as about others. And they begin to view the world with a new lens.

Carl Milofsky
Bucknell University
milofsky@bucknell.edu

I like to assign a "rich" field experience that students undertake on their own initiative and in response to which they write a three page paper describing the experience.

"Rich" refers to a setting that includes multiple sub-groups or subcommunities, interacting together, in a way that is apparent even to beginning students.

The richness of the setting leads nearly all students to come away with particular observations and provocative thoughts they want to talk about. This allows us to talk about what ethnographic observation is and what you are supposed to see when you observe. The contrasting communities or groups present also allows for discussions of particular topics, depending on the setting one chooses.

This week I'm linking it to my textbook discussion of Goffman, the presentation of self, and the social construction of communities. This works because I am sending students to visit rural estate auctions in Pennsylvania. A colleague in Paris (Henri Peretz) sends his students to visit an upper class Catholic Church in central Paris (La Madeleine) that is surrounded by working class vendors' stalls and that creates a complex multi-class interaction pattern. He uses this experience to talk about the way class is manifested in social interaction. One can argue about what exactly constitutes these "rich" settings and ultimately each instructor has to find his or her own. It is important to recognize that many settings one might pick turn out to be "not rich"---street markets in our experience are an example because venders defend themselves against probing questioners and so the settings end up being flat.

Amy Slater
MCC-Blue River
amy.slater@mcckc.edu

I do something called a lifeboat problem. Many people are on a ship and it's going down. The captain stays with the ship but it has to be decided who goes on the lifeboat because there are not enough seats for everyone. The trick is each person has something that someone can make assumptions about...the 75 year old priest, the reformed prostitute, the gay architect, etc...

The class is split up into groups and they must all decide who goes on the lifeboat and why. We then discuss the assumptions they made about the people they put on the boat and those they didn't. We talk about only having limited information about someone and making a decision about their life or character based on that small amount of information. The students seem to love it.

Georgie Ann Weatherby
Gonzaga University
weatherb@gonzaga.edu

On Board, I write three questions: 1.) When you walk down a busy street during the day, how much eye contact do you establish, and with whom? 2.) How about on a less crowded street at night? 3.) Does this vary depending on who you are? And who you encounter? (Hypothesize about other people and their reactions as well...)

Instructions to Students: Divide up into groups of two with someone close by. Face your chairs toward one another. One person will speak at a time—for three **uninterrupted** minutes—**to** the other person. The other is to time them, but to say nothing—not even "uh huh." No reinforcement should be given. (Note: This is **extremely** hard to do!) You will address the three questions on the board related to eye contact—one at a time—in a "free-thinking"/"free-speaking" manner. **Don't** try to address all of the questions on the first "round." After three minutes, switch roles, and do the same thing. Now the **other** person talks. Do this two more times, on **both** sides, to add to your thoughts (each person getting a total of 3 three minute periods to speak)—for 18 minutes in all. Then we'll get back together as a whole and discuss what we came up with. Also, if you were raised in another culture, or have experience in another culture, please feel free to elaborate on your experiences there.

Discussion: How was your own eye contact during your discussion here? And that of your partner? (We tend to cue off of one another.) Continue from there with student feedback on the results of the exercise.

Anne Wortham
Rappahannock Community College
awortham@rcc.vccs.edu

All my students have to do a twenty participant observation in a public place. They then write up the things they observed like they are really sociologists! I have them read them to the class. They are to observe gestures, body language, personal space, clothing, and any norms they can. We then go to having them think up an Unobtrusive Measure that will measure human behavior without anyone knowing they are doing so. This one is really fun and the students get into this. They do not have to do the unobtrusive measure, just think up one and share it with their classmates.

TOPIC SEVEN

Groups and Organizations

William M. Cross
Illinois College
cross@ic.edu

My teaching tactic deals with the Introductory Sociology subtopic, "Small Groups." The question I address is, "How to help students see the problems organizations have?" The answer is, "How groups evolve usable approaches to a specific problem."

Have the class imagine a group that is experiencing a clash between those who organized the group (which was designed at first to help people of different races and ethnic groups to socialize by eating and talking together) and new and recent members who joined the group (and who now want to broaden the group's purpose). The recent and new members want to have guest speakers from groups impaired by problems of limited vision and hearing, the homeless, the unemployed, people who grew up in foster homes, among other things. The founders of the group want to keep it focused only on interracial and ethnic groups, with few guest speakers, and on conversation over dinner, not allowing families with small children to attend. How could the group be helped to include both the founders, and those wanting a broader approach? How could this group move away from conflict over which approach to take?

The class, after the problem is presented to them, could be divided into small groups, with each group asked to work out a solution to the conflict between the two approaches. During the last fifteen minutes or so, a spokesperson for each group would present the solution to the whole class. Part of a second class period could be used to compare and contrast the various solutions presented. Afterward, the class could be divided into small groups, to create a positive solution, drawing from the various presentations given previously.

Sharon Jones
Belhaven College, Jackson, MS
scjones@bellsouth.net

When we study how groups are formed and how the members relate, I put my class into two separate groups and require that the two groups have the responsibility of instructing for an entire class period. The method of instruction and the topic is entirely up to each group. Group dynamics come into play and each student is to relate in writing what the group experience meant to them. It has been very interesting to see the different topics and methods of instruction that the students will use.

William Kornblum
City University of New York
Carolyn D. Smith
Study Guide for Kornblum, 8E, p. 77

Internet Activity

Federal government organizations are being subjected to a great deal of criticism for intelligence failures related to the September 11, 2001, terrorist attacks. Look at some of the following online essays, editorials, and commentaries to deepen your understanding of these debates. infed.org/bornandbred/lead-bk.htm, http://oilempire.us/warnings.html, and http://ppub17.ezboard.com/fhumanrightsfrm18.showMessage? topicID=5.topic

Alicia Lupinacci
Tarrant County College Northwest Campus
alicia.lupinacci@tccd.edu

To help students learn the concept of the term groupthink, I ask for a volunteer to leave the classroom. Then I tell his/her peers that I am going to point to a spot (not really there) that the painters missed when they repainted the room. The students will affirm that they see the spot when I call on them after the one student has rejoined their classmates. Sometimes the student will claim to see the spot which is not really there, and oftentimes they do not. However, the students begin to grasp the concept that several people persuading one person to go along with the crowd can be very strong and influential.

Judith Pintar
University of Illinois at Urbana-Champaign
Brym/Lie Brief 2e IRM, p. 64

Make a list of all of the secondary and primary groups to which you belong. How have these groups changed over time? Do you see yourself belonging to the same primary and secondary groups in five years? Write a short paper explaining your findings.

TOPIC EIGHT

Deviance and Crime

Caroll B. Johnson Hodson
Rowan-Cabarrus Community College
hodgsonc@rowancabarrus.edu

Town Council Meeting

This hypothetical "town" council meeting is a forum for debating topics coming from the sexuality or deviance chapters. The entire class will make up the voting town council as well as a debating group. Usually the entire class is separated into four groups. The goal of each group is to argue its point to try to get its motion passed before the town council.

Suggested topics to debate are:

Pornography:
First Group: This group wants to ban pornography from the town. The problem lies in defining what pornography is. State government gives local towns and cities jurisdiction to define their own decency laws. The goal of this group is to determine what they feel is pornography: topless bars, magazines, videos, etc. In addition, they must specify how they plan to enforce the ban and what consequences will arise from possessing restricted material.

Second Group: The second group is opposed to group one. They should also determine what is indecent and what is not. After their determination they should specify what the town should allow and why. For example, topless bars could bring in revenue and pornographic magazines could satisfy needs and desires for people who do not have partners. I encourage them to use theories like feminist theory or conflict theory to support their arguments. The town council will vote on the group whose arguments were more persuasive.

Prostitution:
First Group: This group wants to legalize prostitution. Their goal is to define why they want to legalize and how they are going to legalize. For example, they may want to legalize because it is a source of revenue and they will only legalize controlled brothels. The purpose is to examine the pros and cons of legalized prostitution. I encourage them to use theory like the feminist theory or conflict theory to support their arguments.

Second Group: The second group is opposed to group one. They should argue why legalizing prostitution would not be beneficial to the town. I encourage them to use theory like the feminist theory or conflict theory to support their arguments. The town council will vote on the group whose arguments were more persuasive.

You can also use the town council meeting to debate other issues like legalization of drugs, lowering the drinking age, etc.

Minu Mathur
College of San Mateo
mathur@smccd.edu

My favorite method of teaching about the characteristics of the prison population (young, male, minority, low-income, low-education), is to start by asking the class whether we have a lot of crime/deviance or little in the U.S. When they reply that we have very high rates, I draw a large circle on the board. Then I start by drawing smaller and smaller circles on the board to indicate that the number of incarcerated gets smaller and smaller since not every crime leads to an arrest, every arrest does not lead to a booking, every booking does not lead to a charge, every charge does not lead to a trial, every trial does not lead to a conviction, every conviction does not lead to incarceration (alternatives, such as fines, restitution, house arrest, may be used). So, the circle gets extremely small by the end. Thus I conclude by highlighting how race, gender, social class, and age of criminals have an impact on incarceration.

Dwaine Plaza
Oregon State University
dplaza@orst.edu

I have my students engage in committing a positive act of kindness to a stranger. After doing this act my students can be able to clearly see one of the cultural "norms" in the United States-- that is a fear for strangers doing kind acts to strangers. Students can also see how positive deviance can be seen as a threat if done within an individual's proximal bubble. We can also talk about gender differences (threatening genders verses non threatening). We can also discuss the importance of attractiveness, "race" etc... as variables which allow some strangers to not be seen as threatening compared to others. It's a great activity to get students engaged and talking in class. Here is the detailed outline to the activity:

Deviance Field Exercise: Generally, when we think of deviance, the word has a negative connotation, and we may think of behaviors such as crime, mental illness, alcoholism, etc. What I would like you to do is to go out and commit a random act of kindness to a stranger—arguably, a form of positive deviance. Many introductory sociology classes ask students to "break a norm" and to observe the reactions of those around them. In this case, I am asking you to perform a face-to-face act of kindness for a stranger and to take note of the reaction to your behavior.

Think about the following questions in completing your act(s) of kindness: (a) Why did you choose to do this particular act of kindness? (b) How did you feel while doing the random act of kindness and why do you think you felt this way? What does this reaction suggest to you about American cultural "norms"? (c) How did the "recipient" and any others who witnessed the act of "kindness" react? Speculate as to why they reacted the way they did? (d) If the situation was reversed and you were the recipient of the act of kindness, do you think you would have reacted differently? Based on these questions and your observations, write a one page summary of your experiment. Describe the scene and the set up for your act of kindness, briefly explain why you decided to do the particular act, and then briefly comment on what you feel you learned about American cultural norms, deviance or social control from this experiment? Be safe and smart in the choice of kindness you do. Be sure to adhere to the ethical treatment of human subjects. This also means to be careful not to inflict physical or mental trauma on yourself or the recipient and be certain that you do not put yourself in a dangerous position at any time.

Nathan W. Pino
Texas State University and
Robert F. Meier
University of Nebraska
IRMTB for Sociology of Deviant Behavior, 13E, p. 60

Mafia: Does the mafia really exist? Some experts question descriptions of such an organization. They characterize the belief in a U.S. Mafia as the result of distortion driven by ulterior motives and sensational reporting. Does the mafia exist in America? Visit the website on "MAFIA." (http://mprofaca.cro.net/orgcrim.html). As a class discussion, group exercise, or individual writing exercise, research three individual, or groups, or families said to have mafia connections. What did you find interesting? How does your finding compare to the information in the text?

TOPIC NINE

Class and Stratification

David J. Ayers
Grove City College
Stark 10e IRM, p. 127

"Are We from Upwardly Mobile Families?"

Have students trace back their forbearer's occupations and education as far back as possible, starting with their parents and then grandparents (most will only get that far). Then discuss this as a class. How many already see a pattern of upward mobility? If they are reasonably successful in their occupational and educational goals, will they be "higher" or "lower" than their parents? How about than their grandparents?

Tracy L. Dietz
University of Central Florida
IRMTB for Brinkerhoff's Essentials of Sociology 7E, p. 96

Internet Exercise

It is always fun to dream about wealth, so have students visit the Forbes website to find the list of the 400 richest Americans (http://forbes.com/400richest) or the list of the world's richest people (http://forbes.com/worldsrichest). Forbes also keeps other lists, for instance the top 100 celebrities, that may also be of interest. Ask students to see how many names they recognize? Do they shop at their stores, buy their gasoline, root for any of their professional sports teams? Ask them also to consider how their own lives would be changed if they were on one of these lists. What would remain the same and what would they do differently?

William J. Elenchin
St. Bonaventure University
welenchi@sbu.edu

In my introduction to sociology course, when presenting a discussion about global wealth and poverty, I engage students in a simple but powerful demonstration. I hand out index cards to 1/5 of my students who represent example nations that compose the richest 20% of humanity (which have 80% of the global income). I then hand out index cards which represent the poorest nations to 1/5 of my students. These nations have 1% of the global population. The remaining represent those who live in between these two extremes, and are given cards which represent example nations. We then discuss how lives may be different for different people, depending on income. To hopefully make an impression, I then hand out three small packages of chocolate bars, which have a ratio of food equal to that of the levels of wealth per income group. The result in my class of approximately 25 students is that those five youngsters who represent the rich nations have a huge bag of chocolate...much more than they can eat. Those students who are the "middle" group (15 students) have a bag that is roughly adequate for everyone to get a piece, yet still much smaller than the richest five. Finally the poorest five students get a bag with one small candy bar to share. Visually this is a very powerful exercise. We then process the activity, making the point that while this is a comfortable college exercise, the reality of poverty is a very real and sobering global problem.

Class and Stratification

Cristina Gordon
Fox Valley Technical College
gordon@fvtc.edu

Social Stratification Activity

Before discussing social stratification, divide the class into four different groups. Each group is to represent a social class. The upper class will have the least amount of people, followed by the middle-upper class with a few more, then the middle class with a lot more, and finally the lower class with the most number of members in the group. Provide each group with their "resources" and explain these resources must be shared by the group. Give the upper class group a box with 48 crayons; the upper-middle class a box with 24 crayons; the middle class a box with 8 crayons, and the lower class 3 crayons (brown, black and red). Distribute blank pieces of paper to each individual and tell them to draw their dream home, with all the colors and amenities (correctly colored, such as grass, pool, etc) they want. They must share their resources. Meanwhile, tape on the wall titles for the social classes. Once students are done drawing, place their drawings under the appropriate title for their social class. Discuss as a group what the differences are and what the reasons are for those differences. Themes that may arise are:

-Different resources.
-Number of people sharing resources.
-Few colors, not able to produce a lawn or a pool for example.

Following the discussion, introduce the topic on social stratification.

Jerry Jo Manfred-Gilham
Franciscan University of Steubenville
jgilham@franciscan.edu

When discussing class and dealing with poverty, we examine the worthy v. the unworthy. We also discuss whether one is poor due to character flaws (laziness) or structural factors (lack of good jobs or lack of training). With these things in mind, we then look at the lifestyle of a mom receiving public assistance. For instance, we figure out her monthly income and then look at her expenses (rent, utilities, clothes, recreation, transportation, food, etc), and students are often very surprised at how little she actually has to meet her needs. We then look at a mom who is making minimum wage and working 32 hours per week. We then look at her income and expenses, which are greater now that she has to pay for child care, and work related expenses including transportation and clothes. We find that she is not faring much better even though she is working nearly full time. We then discuss the fact that she is working outside the home for little increase in income and someone else is now caring for her children. This exercise is enlightening for students. I shared it with another faculty member and he too uses it with intro students. I use it with my social work students also.

Lucy Ogburn
Middlesex Community College
ogburnl@middlesex.mass.edu

Students read several articles on the wealth and income gap in the United States. Then, they divide into groups and discuss the major causes and consequences of the gap. Next, they plan for a round table discussion of the issues raised in the articles.

Class and Stratification

They are instructed to take on roles that represent people and points of view on all sides of the gap. I tell them to pretend that they are on an in-depth news program. The roles that they play range from the news hosts to corporate executive, U.S. congressman, low wage worker, welfare social worker, middle income worker, educator, etc. Then they develop a script for each role that encompasses the issues that particular person faces and represents in the wealth/income gap. I also do this same type of exercise using Wal-Mart. I show them a film on Wal-Mart and they do research on its effects on society. They role play various people responding to the question "Is Wal-Mart good for America?" Roles may include a Wal-Mart executive, a Wal-Mart worker, someone in a town who opposes a new Wal-Mart being built, a consumer who likes shopping there, a small store owner threatened by Wal-Mart, a union organizer, etc. I encourage them to come to class on the day of the role play dressed for their role.

Bob Transon
Milwaukee Area Technical College
transonr@matc.edu

Discuss the differences between the words prejudice, discrimination, and racism; give an example in your life when you have been discriminated against and what your prejudices are. Divide the class into groups and have them discuss the terms and how they have been discriminated against and what prejudices they have. Have the group pick out the best or most usual ones and report on them.

TOPIC TEN

Race and Ethnicity

Ron J. Hammond
Utah Valley State College
IMTB for Marger, 7E, p. 12

Ask students to list the education level and class standing of their parents, and all four grandparents. Ask them to estimate their own education level and class standing once they are established in their chosen career. Will they experience intergenerational mobility? Does race, class, gender, lifestyle, or disability impact their findings? Did race, class, gender, lifestyle, or disability impact their parents' and grandparents' educational and class experience?

Jill Harrison
Rhode Island College
jharrison@ric.edu

I ask students to pick three "Top Ten" songs off any billboard/chart and analyze their content for sociological concepts. We develop the hypotheses to test in class, so the class tests all the same items. For example, in an introductory sociology class, we can use the themes of race, class, and gender to analyze the content and link them with C. Wright Mills, Marx, etc. Hypotheses are student generated, so they will vary. For example, to test a Marxian concept about inequality, one hypothesis might be, "Women are more likely to be victimized in song lyrics than are men." "Victimization"

is carefully defined in class. This initial hypothesis can also be expanded to include dimensions of race and class. Students are taught to code the data and create a table. Then they must write a paper that addresses the theory, the data, their analysis, and conclusions. It's a good length for introductory students and gets them using material they are comfortable with while covering all the bases: scientific method, qualitative data analysis, theory, and application of theory, and an original analysis. Students seem to enjoy it!
Cross-referenced with sociological perspectives and research methods.

Shirley A. Jackson
Southern Connecticut State University
jacksons1@southernct.edu

For years, whenever I discuss stereotyping in my introductory sociology course, I place ethnic names on the board and then ask the students to tell me about each person based only on the name. After they have come up with a list of characteristics for each name, I tell them that I personally know each of the people listed. I then go through each list and check off those things that I know are true about the person and those that are not. The only thing that the students usually get correct is the race/ethnicity of the individual. It's a good way to teach them about stereotyping and how this may lead to prejudice depending on the person who sees or hears each of the names written on the board.

Karla M. McLucas
Bennett College for Women
kmclucas@bennett.edu

Affordable housing challenge.

I divide students into several teams based on scenarios. For example, one team may be a young married couple, another a multi-generational family, another an aged out of foster care couple expecting a child. The teams are given varying amounts of down-payment and a household budget. Their task is to locate a place to live with a manageable mortgage. The students present the outcome of their project to the entire class, which leads to fascinating discussions about gender, race, and the wealth gap challenges in this country.
Cross-referenced with gender and stratification.

Vincent G. Thomas
Black Hawk College
vgthomas@qconline.com

In my first introductory class I write my name and ask a question. "What kind of Indian am I?" I am originally from India. I am dark skinned and balding. I wear a cap that says "Native American" or another which is obviously Native American designed with bead work and a white bison. I wear a bolo tie which has an arrowhead on it. I ask the students to write their first impressions of me and try to answer the question. After I collect the 2X5 cards I had distributed for answers, I explain some (very few) of the students correctly identify me with India (generally they are students who are nurses or those who have had contact with Asian Indian doctors). Most of the students are unsure of my true background. I begin to explain how we learn to form impressions of others, based on names (Thomas is a familiar South-Indian Christian name) the Vincent comes from my mother's side of the family (she was from Goa--Catholics.) So even though my name is very American, it was created in India. I belong to a Native American coalition here and have received my adornments as gifts. So this is an icebreaker for me, because now I ask the students to write their backgrounds on another set of 2x5 cards for me. Then I ask them to pair off and talk about themselves briefly to one another. Some of the information they have given me about themselves I share at the second class, such as how many nurses, veterans, where they came from originally, etc. are present and what the goals of the students are without revealing personal information they may have written about themselves. We all learn from this experience that we are an interconnected society with many common goals even though some live in the cities and some are from rural towns. This experience is also a new experience in communicating with people they may never have had the opportunity to do so before and learn about their cultural backgrounds. Of course, all this does not happen instantaneously in the first class. But the communication and learning from one another continues throughout the course. We relate our interconnectedness to current events.

Cross-referenced with General Teaching Tactics.

Shiela Venkataswamy
McHenry County College
svenkata@mchenry.edu

Using M&M's to Explain Discrimination

One idea for the chapter on Race and Ethnicity is using M & M's to explain the related concepts. Dr. Marilyn Kern Foxante in her poem "Me and My M&M's", states that they are the most diverse multicultural integrated candy in the world. All of us, however, have discriminated our M & M's as children. Some of us may continue to do so. We have our favorites, which are saved for the last in spite of them all being the same on the inside! The requirement for this venture is M&M's (regular and with peanuts). Ask students how they ate their M&M's as children. Students may state their preference for certain colors, presence or absence of "m" and shape of the candy. This can direct to an introduction of the concept of salience principle, which is the basis of stereotypes, prejudice, and discrimination, which is what we do when we prefer certain M&M's or refuse to eat certain colors. The lecture/discussion can end with students feasting on the M&M's indiscriminately!

Reference: Dr. Kern Foxante, Marilyn. "Me and My M&M's." Poetry. 29 Jun. 2007
http://diversity.ucf.edu/clearing_house/poetry.htm#me.

TOPIC ELEVEN

Sex and Gender

Claudia Chaufan
University of California Santa Cruz
claudiachaufan@yahoo.com

1) Teaching gender stereotypes: I ask my students if they believe that the United States has achieved a fair degree of gender equality, if not in pay (which by now they read is not the case), at least in access to education and in social norms constraining the behavior of men and women (e.g. sexual behaviors). Depending on the student audience, by and large the answer is affirmative. Then I ask students to pair up and write two lists, one with words they know for "women who sleep around" and one with words they know for "men who sleep around". I ask them to simply note the number of words they find to list under each category. Last, I use either a show of hands, or in large classes (only once) Personal Response System with three options, asking students if 1) their list for men was longer 2)their list for women was longer 3)they found no significant difference (or are undecided, or do not wish to answer). I've only done it once with PRS in a class of 400 students, which unsurprisingly replicated the more anecdotal results of smaller classes. The impact on my students, especially of the contrast between their answer to the first and second question, is always profound. I use this as a springboard to discuss further the question of stereotypes, and norms, more generally.

2) Teaching about same-sex marriage: To clarify the confusion in debates about same sex marriage, I work on the meaning of the concept of "definition". Although this pertains to the field of philosophy, that I have a background in, I believe that this clarification has important implications for the same-sex marriage debate in the sociological / legal arena. I begin by asking students what is the definition of bachelor, or what they would find if they look the word bachelor up in the dictionary. They all say something close to "unmarried man". Then I ask them to imagine if it would be possible to pass a law determining that from now on bachelors can remain bachelors even if they marry. They typically look at me thinking that I lost my mind, and say that this is of course impossible (although some student may want to play clever and say yes, but then I follow up until they give up). So I ask them why this is not possible. They are even more puzzled. Then I clarify that such a law would change the definition of bachelor, which is not something that laws typically do (we have more important things to legislate about than the definition of words). Definitions change with use, and when new uses of words become established as a result of social practices they are (or not) introduced in the dictionary. So, saying that a bachelor can be a bachelor and married at the same time is self contradictory, a logical impossibility. If accepted, such change would destroy the definition of bachelor. Then I move on to marriage, and give them the definition used by sociologists and anthropologists, "a group's approved mating arrangements, usually marked by a ritual of sorts". Then I cite several historical examples about such arrangements, beginning with King David in the Bible, following with Common Law marriage, and the time when it was no longer recognized (mid 1700s), followed by mating arrangements in various countries in the Middle East, and

ending by the legalization of same sex marriage in the Netherlands in 2001. Then I ask students what happened with the definition of marriage each time a new or different rule came to regulate the social institution. The answer is obviously nothing because marriage is defined by a rule, a norm or a law, that does not specify who the participants in the arrangements are (if they fail to see it I go back to the definition I gave them before, or have them look it up in the glossary of their intro books). I conclude by suggesting that the claim that legalizing same-sex marriage would redefine marriage because "marriage is defined between a man and a woman", as public figures often claim, is literally non-sense, that is, it makes no sense, it cannot be said to be true or false. This of course does not mean that such change in the legislation would be good or bad, or whatever the debate might be. But the case for badness (or goodness) needs to be made, providing good reasons and relevant evidence and conclusions that follow from the premises, i.e., the fundamental elements of sound arguments.

Monica Edwards
Loyola University Chicago
medwarl@luc.edu

In learning about gender socialization, I show my Introduction to Sociology students an episode of the television show, Friends (The One Where Rachel Goes Back to Work; 9th Season). The students come to class having read the article, "Night to His Day: The Social Construction of Gender" by Judith Lorber. I give my students an outline of what I expect them to look for/think about while watching the episode, making connections between the article and the television show (e.g. what scenarios are illustrative of gender socialization? What agents of socialization are exemplified in the episode? How do these scenarios help us to see/articulate that gender is a social construct? How is difference being constructed in this episode?). We then discuss the article, and illuminate the sociological perspective, using the show as a tool to exemplify the process, and as a shared discussion point. It also becomes a basis to discuss how the mass media is involved as an agent of socialization. The students report enjoying watching the show (even with its shortcomings); it breaks up the lectures, and it is, for many students, funny. Given that the show is a comedy, and based on other factors of the shows demographics, it is also a good way to help develop critical thinking skills. Further, we can begin to explore a topic that for some is sensitive, or that challenges their pre-existing ideas, with a common base of examples to utilize.

Kristie A. Ford
Skidmore College
kford@skidmore.edu

"FORCED CHOICES" EXERCISE

Objectives:
To engage students with sociological concepts and/or theories in an interactive way
To encourage thoughtful self-reflection and intergroup discussion
To bring awareness to student's own preconceptions, values, and beliefs

Preparation:
Time allotment: 20 minutes (as an "icebreaker" exercise); 30-45 minutes (to allow for more in-depth discussion)

Sex and Gender

Materials needed: Large open area that permits students to move around freely; list of "forced choices" statements

"Forced Choices" Statements: These statements can vary widely depending upon the sociological concepts you are covering for that particular class period. Below are some sample statements I created to help students think more critically about various theoretical perspectives of gender:

o Men and women are fundamentally the same and should be treated exactly the same.
o It is possible to meet people and not notice and/or ascribe a gender to them.
o Boys are naturally more aggressive than girls.
o Gender difference is an outcome of gender inequality.
o Gender is a context and time dependent performance.
o Gender is largely determined by a person's physical anatomy and hormones.
o Gender is fluid and malleable.
o Children are born gender neutral and learn sex roles early in life.
o Gender is a combination of nature and nurture.
o Gender is rooted in our psyche.
o Gender is socially determined and cannot exist outside of social interaction.

Instructions:

On the left side of the black board, write "agree" and on the right side of the board, write "disagree."
Ask students to stand up and push the desks to the perimeter of the room.

Explain to the students that you will read a series of statements. After the statement is read, students should silently move to the left side of the room if they "agree" with the statement and to the right if they "disagree."
Inform them that there is no "neutral" position – in other words, they are forced to make a choice.
The instructor should read the first statement and ask the students to move to the appropriate side of the room. Pause. Ask one or two students on each side to explain why they moved to the left or right. Allow a few minutes for discussion and then move on to the next statement. Repeat as time permits.

Debriefing Questions:
What are your initial reactions to this activity?
What statements were easy? More challenging? Why?
What did you learn about yourself during this activity? What values inform your position?
What did you learn about others? Were there any surprises?
How does activity connect to the readings for today? How does this activity connect to our previous conversations in this course?

NOTE: I often do this activity twice –once in the beginning of the semester and then again at the end of the semester. By the end of the semester, students should have a more nuanced understanding of the sociological concepts and theories, enabling the class to move to a deeper level of analysis and discussion.
Cross-referenced with General Teaching Tactics

Sex and Gender

Robert Gellman
Kansas State University
Lecture Ideas for Courses on the Family, Vol 1, p. 25

To demonstrate that traditional gender role expectations are more strict for men than for women: Ask students to provide you with adjectives and labels given to a male adolescent who does not participate in sports, enjoys things like theatre and fashion and is sensitive. (Students will use words like fag, queer, fairy, pussy, wuss, etc.). Then, ask students to identify words and labels for a female adolescent who is athletic, tough, and not terribly concerned about her clothes and appearance. (Students will mention "tom-boy," but will usually struggle for other adjectives.) Point out how difficult it is for men in our society to break from the traditional, instrumental male gender role.

Dana Hysock
University of Delaware
IMTB for Andersen and Hill Collins's Race, Class, and Gender: An Anthology, 6E, p.3

Role-Taking for Men: How to Put Yourself in the Place of Women in "Role-Taking for Men," female students instruct male students on how to sit, bend, run, and walk as females are often socialized to do. Additional behaviors can be included, such as games females learn to play growing up, how females are told to interact with males, and goals females are encouraged to attain. The male students are then given a chance to practice these behaviors. These exercises were adapted from Nancy Henley's Body Politics (1977). The exercise can also be extended to have the males in the class teach the females how to act out the same behaviors.

Donald Malone
Saint Peter's College
dmalone@spc.edu

In-Class Demonstration

Gender Differences and Body Language

One of the most popular classroom demonstrations I use illustrating gender differences is through the use of body language. I begin by sitting down and crossing my legs knee over knee and I ask if it is "okay" to sit like this. Usually one or two of the males say it is "gay" to sit that way. Other males say they would feel uncomfortable sitting like that. I then ask the females if they would feel comfortable crossing their legs with one leg over one knee – assuming they were wearing jeans or slacks. Some say it is okay, others say they would be uncomfortable. We explore some of the reasons behind their answers.

Next, I ask for a couple of volunteers (male and female) to come to the front of the class to help me demonstrate gender differences in body language. First, I ask the couple to hold hands as a typical couple might do walking down the street. Next, I ask them to reverse the way in which they are holding hands. The female's hand is now "on top" or on the "outside." The class starts to laugh. I ask why they think it looks so "funny." I let them make a few comments. Most say it just seems so "weird." They say they would not do it because it would make them feel uncomfortable. Then I ask the couple to walk arm-in-arm as a couple. The female inserts her arm around the males' arm. I ask them to reverse this body language. When the class sees the male holding onto his female companion's arm, they erupt into laughter as if this is just too much to bear. Again, I ask why this appears so funny or strange to them. After some discussion, one or more students may comment that men are expected to "protect" women and that maybe this body language reflects that.

We then begin a discussion of "gender" and what that term means sociologically speaking. We explore issues of power, dominance and control that may be embedded in the body language we examined. We also question if these forms of body language are simply holdovers from another male dominated era. However, this discussion is a good way to explore male dominance in the workplace, politics and the family.

Etsuko Maruoka
Suffolk Country Community College
maruoke@sunysuffolk.edu

The purposes of this exercise are: 1) to increase students' understanding of gender socialization; 2) to learn the basic research methods in sociology; and 3)to apply the three basic sociological perspectives in real life settings.

First, I give my students the following assignment. In the following class I make them compare their findings and analysis. At the last half of the class time period, I facilitate a discussion on the three points described above.

Assignment: "One must learn by doing the thing, for though you think you know it - you have no certainty until you try." - Sophocles (BC 495-406) Do one of the following two exercises.

OPTION 1:

1. Go to a toy store in your local area. By using the technique of Observational Research, observe and describe how the boys' and girls' sections are different by focusing on the following criteria:

    a. What kinds of things are displayed and sold in each section?

    b. What kinds of words or phrases are used to describe the toys in each section?

    c. What colors and decorations are used in each section?

    d. What sounds do those toys make?

    e. Where are those toys meant to be played with?

2. Based on your field notes, analyze and discuss why you think there are differences by using one of the following sociological perspectives introduced in class and textbook – i.e. Structural-Functionalism, Conflict Theory, and Symbolic Interactionism.

OPTION 2:

1. Select a film that is produced for children from the list on the back side. By using the technique of Content Analysis, describe it by focusing on the following criteria:

    a. Who are the characters and what are their demographic characteristics – i.e. gender, age, class, etc.?

    b. What themes about gender does it include?

    c. How does the film convey dominant societal values and norms based on gender? What are they?

    d. How do the visual images, such as the characters' physical figure, kinds of clothes and colors that they put on, and gestures that they use, support the gender norms and values?

Sex and Gender

2. Analyze and discuss what lesson boys and girls who watch the film learn by using one of the following sociological perspectives introduced in class and textbook – i.e. Structural-Functionalism, Conflict Theory, and Symbolic Interactionism.

Film List - Aladdin - Batman - Beauty and Beast - Cinderella - Hercules - Snow White and the Seven Dwarfs - Spiderman - Superman - The Little Mermaid - The Sword in the Stone - The Lion King - Tarzan
Cross referenced with research methods and sociological perspectives.

TOPIC TWELVE

Aging and Age-Based Inequality

Shelley Brown
Tennessee Technological University
csbrown@tntech.edu

When we get to the chapter on Gerontology and Aging, I use an "Aging Sensitivity Workshop". This is a hands-on activity in which the students divide up into groups of 2-3 and visit various stations I have prepared in the classroom. The stations are designed to illustrate various physical aspects of aging such as loss of dexterity, loss of vision, loss of hearing, decreased taste. For decreased taste, the students are blindfolded and cotton put in their nose, and asked to taste baby food. They experience how smell and texture aid in food identification and taste. For dexterity, the students use an ace bandage or tape around joints and try to pick up small objects, or unscrew a jar or medicine bottle. For blurred vision the students wear goggles sprayed with hairspray and attempt to read fine print or a newspaper. For tunnel vision the students wear goggles with the fronts colored in black except for a small circle in the very front. For loss of hearing, the students wear earplugs while 2 other students give them instructions for a simple activity, or they can try to follow the instructions while a radio is also playing. I also create other stations to illustrate loss of balance and decreased sense of touch depending on time and class size. At the end, we discuss how our society views the aged versus how other societies view the aged.

Aging and Age-Based Inequality

David Knox
East Carolina University
Knox 9e IRM/TB, p. 392

Invite students from other cultures to talk to the class about a) how the elderly are viewed and treated in their native culture and b) the role of the elderly in the family in their native culture.

D.R. Wilson
Houston Baptist University
IRM for Kendall's Sociology in Our Times, 6E, p. 256

Suggest that students examine advertisements for retirement communities and services especially geared for older persons. How realistic are their claims about the "golden years" of retirement? Encourage students to analyze advertisements, television shows, or movies for depictions of older persons. How frequently are they depicted? What kinds of roles do they have? In advertisements, what products are they selling?

TOPIC THIRTEEN

Politics and the Economy

Jan Abu-Shakrah
Portland Community College
Andersen/Taylor 4e IRM, p. 224

Use work-related policies of your college or university to illustrate how such policies are implemented and how they affect work organization and experience. Examples of policies include equal employment and affirmative action policies, sexual harassment policies, occupational safety and health, and how the institution is implementing the Americans with Disability Act.

Jan Abu-Shakrah
Portland Community College
Andersen/Taylor 4e IRM, p. 237

Participatory Politics.

Invite organizers or activists from alternative local parties or interest groups that represent participatory politics to talk about how they organize and try to influence the political process and promote their issues. Some of these groups may operate on your campus.

Politics and the Economy

Lori Ann Fowler
Tarrant County College
Study Guide for Mooney's Understanding Social Problems,
5E, p. 106-107

What is that job worth? Individual Activity

Visit the following website:
http://www.bls.gov/oco/ocos074.htm. Select an occupation
that you have an interest in. Use this information to answer the
following questions: 1. What is your occupation? What is the
nature of your work? What are your working conditions?
What training is required for your current occupation?
Describe your job outlook. 2. What is your annual income, as
listed on the website? Remember-Gross Income is not Net
income. What do you think your take home pay might be? 3.
Based on this income, and your lifestyle, design a realistic
expense budget: a) What type of house will you be able to
afford? Where? b) What type of car will you drive? What is
the cost of this vehicle? c) Will you have children? How
many? d) What might you not be able to afford, because of
your occupational choice? e) Based on your occupational
choice, do you think you may have school loans that will need
to be paid off?

D.R. Wilson
Houston Baptist University
IRM for Kendall's Sociology in Our Times: The Essentials,
5E, p. 278

Writing in Sociology: Start class with ten minutes of writing.
1) Are there lessons that we in the United States might learn
from the EU experience? 2) Do you think that there will be
more or less cooperation among the nations of the world in the
future? Explain your answer.

TOPIC FOURTEEN

Families/Intimate Relationships

Caroll B. Johnson Hodson
Rowan-Cabarrus Community College
hodgsonc@rowancabarrus.edu

Homosexual Marriage: Separate the class into groups of four to five people. Give the class the hypothetical idea that the federal government has given local governments power to legalize homosexual marriage. The groups will be looking at this controversial issue from several facets.

First, much of the debate over homosexual marriage is centered on defining it as "marriage". Many people are opposed, not to homosexuals having some sort of union, but to referring to it as "marriage". On the other hand, members of the homosexual community feel they should be granted the same rights as everyone else. Some feel a civil union, even with the same rights, is not equal.

The purpose of the group is to pretend the town they are living in is going to legalize homosexual marriage but they do not want to refer to it as marriage. They should come up with terms beyond marriage and civil union to refer to all licensed marriages within the fictitious town. These terms should be created to appeal to members of both communities.

In addition, groups should specify what duties and rewards should be present in their new "marriage". For example, tax benefits, health and life insurance, economics, power arrangements, childcare etc.

After the groups finish the assignment, have each group address their answers to the entire class and begin a class discussion on which answer would most likely appeal to people.

Donald Malone
Saint Peter's College
dmalone@spc.edu

Homework Writing Assignment

Choosing a Mate

Who marries whom? How do we choose a mate? What are the most important factors people consider in choosing a mate? In the United States, unlike some other countries, there is a strong belief in individual choice in choosing a mate. Does that mean that Americans choose a mate solely on the basis of personal preference? One way to examine this question is to look at engagement and wedding announcements. If we analyze the information provided in these announcements, we may find what factors people consider important in choosing a mate.

Your task is to examine several engagement or wedding announcements to see if you can find clues about preferences in choosing a mate.

Do the following:

1. Find a newspaper or other source that has a listing of engagement or wedding announcements.
2. Read at least five of these announcements and see if you can find any similarities between those getting married. Describe these similarities.

3. Based on the information you analyzed, what patterns did you find? Explain.

4. What differences did you find between these couples? Describe these differences.

5. Explain what you learned about who marries whom from these announcements? Provide examples.

6. Does this confirm or contradict what you believed before you did this research? Explain.

7. Finally, identify the source of your announcement (e.g., newspaper, magazine, on-line etc...) Who do you think its readers are? In other words, what is their background? Would this affect who advertises an engagement or wedding announcement and what kind of information is presented? What do you think? Explain.

This writing assignment should be two pages long and typed, double-spaced and in 12 point font.

Tina Mougouris
San Jacinto College—Central
Tina.Mougouris@sjcd.edu

Before I start the chapter on Love, I have my students take out a blank sheet of paper and write down their definition of love. I also ask for their gender, age and relationship status (married, single, divorced). I then read each of these definitions to the class and we discuss if there are gender differences in terms of how love is defined (it's great for discussing the "feminization of love"). Does one's relationship status impact one's definition? Age? We get lots of great discussions going with this simple exercise.

Cynthia K. Shinabarger Reed
Tarrant County College
Strong 10e IRM/TB, P. 119

Role Play: Pick two students to role-play a jealous couple.
Create a scenario in which one partner has formed a friendship
with a person of the other sex and the other partner is
extremely jealous. Have the couple "discuss" this issue for
about five minutes. Afterwards, each partner should describe
his or her feelings during the encounter. The class can then
discuss jealousy: Is it a natural part of love? What does it
mean? How does it influence a relationship?

D.R. Wilson
Houston Baptist University
IRM for Kendall's Sociology in Our Times, 6E, p. 328

Marriage in Multicultural Perspective

Address the different ways that people organize their families.
Examine stark differences such as Navajo families that are
strongly matriarchal with the traditional patriarchialism of
Mexican families. What factors have contributed to the
development of American families as more egalitarian? Rely
upon the experiences of students in your class who are from
different cultural backgrounds.

TOPIC FIFTEEN

Education and Religion

Jan AbuShakrah
Portland Community College
Andersen/Taylor 4e Ess IRM, p. 165

School Dropouts.

Visit the U.S. Department of Education website (www.ed.gov),
your state Department of Education, and the Education
Commission of the States under At Risk/Dropouts
(www.ecs.org). What are the dropout rates in your state and the
nation, and who are the most likely to drop out? What policies
have proven effective in lowering dropout rates and increasing
student achievement? Participate in the discussion, using
research evidence to support your contribution, and respond to
the input of other students.

David J. Ayers
Grove City College
Stark 10e IRM, p. 180

"Are the Networks Really Less Supportive of Religion on TV
These Days?"

Assign students to watch a spectrum of new television shows,
and re-runs from various time periods. You may wish to focus
on those that you could expect might have more religious
content, such as sitcoms and family dramas. Have students
look for references to religion, and indicate if they are positive
(for example, prayers over dinners or ministers helping people)

or negative (for example, religious hypocrites or bigots). Have them report on how references to religion on such shows changed over time, if at all.

Katheryn A. Dietrich
IRMTB for Mooney's Understanding Social Problems, 5E, 338

The Effects of the School Environment on the Individual

Write two headings on the board: On the left, write "Person A" and on the right, write "Person B." Tell the students that you are going to introduce them to two high school students: Person A and Person B.

Present the following descriptions:

Person A: Hates school, frequently skips classes, flunks some classes, including sophomore English, has few friends in school, must retake sophomore English in summer school, and quits school in the second week of their junior year.

Person B: Loves school, never skips classes, excels in every class, has many friends in school, graduates early, with various honors and awards.

Now, ask students to describe Person A's personal characteristics and likely future situation and write their responses on the board.

Students usually describe Person A as unmotivated, lazy, stupid, irresponsible, etc. and foresee future unemployment, criminal behavior, drug/alcohol abuse, divorce, etc. Then, ask students to describe Person B's characteristics and likely future. The evaluations and future predictions of Person B are typically very positive. Then have the students discuss possible external social factors (school, peers, neighborhood, family SES) that might have affected these students.

Finally, tell students that Person A and Person B are the same person. Explain that this exercise is based on the real life story of the textbook co-author (C. Schacht) for Mooney's *Understanding Social Problems*, who, after quitting high school in her junior year visited an "alternative" high school where she subsequently enrolled. The school was small (a total of 60 students in grades 7 - 12) and class sizes ranged from 1 to about 10. The school was furnished with sofas, lounge chairs, and round tables with chairs instead of traditional desks. Instead of earning grades, students wrote self-evaluation reports for each course they took, describing why they took the course, what they learned in the course, and how many points they think they have earned in the course (4 points = full credit for successful completion of course; 5 or 6 points = outstanding performance in course; 1 to 3 points = less than full credit for course). Class offerings were diverse, and included standard high school fare such as chemistry, U.S. history, and English composition as well as unusual courses such as "Piaget and Winnie the Pooh," "Wild Foods," and "Workshop in Creative Expression." Further, the school was run democratically. Students were invited to participate in faculty meetings and vote on policies concerning such issues as rules about smoking, fund raising events, and disciplinary procedures for rule violations. A student's vote carried the same weight as the school director's vote.

In conclusion, emphasize to students that although they described Person A and Person B as radically different people, the person was the same—only the context changed: the school environment. Person A was in a large, impersonal, authoritarian school that bred alienation; Person B was in a small, personal, democratic school that empowered students and attended to their individual needs. This example also illustrates the sociological imagination in suggesting that students are products of their social context.

Thomas W. Segady
Stephen F. Austin State University
tsegady@sfasu.edu

For my religion section, I differentiate 'sects' from 'cults' by giving examples of each. For sects, I illustrate their 'deviation' from the norms with a small video on the Amish. For 'cults,' I illustrate with a small video on the Jim Jones cult. However, I emphasize that, in investigating any religious group, sociologists must remain value-free. The illustration of this is to apply the characteristics of cults (charismatic leader, opposition to dominant social norms, predominantly achieved membership) to major religions. Both Christianity and Islam, for example, qualify as having begun their existence as 'cults' using these characteristics.

Michael E. Weissbuch
Xavier University
weissbuc@xavier.edu

In the ethnographic research, the student must choose a religious group different from their own, visit services two to three times, do interviews and participant observation. They get permission to attend by simply calling the religious venue and letting them know they are interested in attending and viewing the proceedings. Most churches, synagogues, mosques, etc., are very welcoming. The students observe and take detailed notes on EVERYTHING they see and experience - from the types of cars in the parking lot to the edifice where the service is held and the service itself. From all the information they collect they try to construct a socioeconomic picture of the religious group and interpret what they have experienced in the service. Students are encouraged to compare/contrast the experience with their own religious background and experiences. While the exercise plays fast and loose with the ethnographic concept, it really allows the students to get out of the classroom, use skills we have been working on throughout the course and have some fun. They typically exceed expectations - often including photos and very in-depth interviews with congregants. Most conclude their papers with statements about how "eye-opening" the experience was and how it made them really think about their own religious experiences.

D.R. Wilson
Houston Baptist University
IRM for Kendall's Sociology in Our Times, 6E, p. 377

Religion and Terrorism

Investigate the historical and cross cultural links between religion and the use of violent terror. Help your students to gain some perspective on the current wave of Islamic related terrorism occurring. What we are today calling terrorism in some form or another can be found tied to most of the major world religions at one time in their history.

TOPIC SIXTEEN

Health, Health Care, Disability

Jan AbuShakrah
Portland Community College
Andersen/Taylor 4e IRM, p. 251

Sick Role and Stigma.

Have students write a reflective paper about their personal
experience with the social construction of health, illness, and
the sick role. Did they experience stigma or other forms of
blaming the victim? How was their illness labeled, and what
effect did the label have on how they were treated and how
they felt about their illness and themselves?

Laura Garcia
Washington State Community College
lgarcia@wscc.edu

My SOCI250 cross-cultural communication course seemed
very text-based. I wanted to add something for the kinesthetic
learner. In the health communication module which studies
how different co-cultures in America use healing techniques,
we discuss Navajo sand paintings. After showing a brief video
and handing out a list of symbols drawn from many
southwestern Native American cultures, the students are
required to make a sand painting showing an aspect of their life
which they wish to heal. They can use particle board and sand
- closest to the real thing - or any medium. Some choose
PowerPoint or a Word document, some hand draw using
crayons, paint or markers on posters, while others have created

a three dimensional view (many Native American cultures view the world as north, south, east, west, up, and down). The students have to research the symbols further and include a reflection entry on the representation in their work. Many have commented that this was the most intriguing module. This activity is also assigned in my online class. The students can upload either the Word document/PowerPoint or upload a picture of the finished product.

Nathan W. Pino
Texas State University
and Robert F. Meier
University of Nebraska
IRMTB for Sociology of Deviant Behavior, 13E, p. 117

InfoTrac Exercise

Mentally retarded people do not learn as quickly as non-retarded people do, nor do they retain as much information as others do. What causes mental retardation? As a class discussion, group exercise, or individual writing exercise, research mental retardation. Using InfoTrac College Edition, search the keywords "mental retardation." What are some causes of mental retardation? What are some treatment avenues for mental retarded individuals? Answer these questions by giving synopses on three different articles about mental retardation.

TOPIC SEVENTEEN

Population and Urbanization

David J. Ayers
Grove City College
Stark 10e IRM, p. 242

"What's Better, Cities, Suburbs, or Small Town / Rural Areas?"

Have your students write down which of the above three types of locations they would prefer to live in, and at which stage of life - for example, as a young single, newly married, married with children, older or "empty nest." For each stage, they should indicate the reasons for their location preferences. (Of course, they may believe that they will just prefer one type of location at every stage of their lives, in which case they should indicate that and why, unless they'd like to deal with each stage separately.) Then discuss student answers.

John R. Weeks
San Diego State University
Online IMTB for Week's Population, 10E.

The United Nations Children's Fund (UNICEF) maintains a database for all countries in which you can obtain a profile of the basic indicators of the life chances of the average child. Go to: http://www.unicef.org/statistics/index.html and click on "Country Statistics." Compare Ghana and Egypt on the following measures: (1) adult literacy for females; (2) calculate the ratio of male adult literacy to female adult literacy; (3) child marriages in rural areas; and (4) percent of the population living on less than $1 per day, and (5) one more variable that grabs your attention. Discuss what these results mean for the life chances in each country, and then speculate about reasons for differences between the two countries.

TOPIC EIGHTEEN

Collective Behavior and Social Change

Caroll B. Johnson Hodson
Rowan-Cabarrus Community College
hodgsonc@rowancabarrus.edu

The purpose of this assignment is to introduce students to social movements. Students should get into groups of four to five people. While in groups, students should bring an issue to light they believe should be made into a social movement. Once they decide what issues should be turned into a social movement decide what type of social movement it may fall into as far as how much change and who will be changed. For example, are the social movements alterative, redemptive, reformative, and revolutionary? Once the issue is defined, students should decide which audience to target and how to target the audience. In other words, how will they get organized? After the groups finish the assignment have each group address their answers to the entire class and begin a class discussion on which social movement would most likely appeal to people.

Judith Pintar
University of Illinois at Urbana-Champaign
Brym/Lie 3e IRM, p. 307

To students:

Pretend to see something in the sky outside. Point up to it and observe the different ways that people respond to it collectively. Recruit some friends to help you. Document the reactions with video and write up your observations in a short paper.

John T. Robich
Richmond Community College
johnr@richmondcc.edu

Over many years using Joan Ferrante's *Sociology: A Global Perspective*, I require students to construct a Global Sociology Journal newspaper scrapbook which minimally includes each of the countries cited in all 16 chapters, or a Multinational Corporation (for Ch. 6) or a Social Change focus article for Ch. 16. Newspapers are made available for students to clip articles from weeded copies supplied by the campus library. Each article must be mounted on the journal page, with a title of the country (or multinational or social change concept) at the top, some brief explanation of the global interdependence connection, and any supporting add-ons relating to that country/society (e.g. Gaza Strip is a society, but not a country, from Ch. 3). Students will post stamp, menu, currency, flag, map partition. The student must organize/format a complete Table of Contents, Title Page, and Newspaper reference page. Virtually all students exceed the Ferrante countries, and have compiled Journals with 50, 100, to as many as 300-400 pages of country/society info. The title must read: MY GLOBAL SOCIOLOGY JOURNAL PROJECT. Many students have enthusiastically and gratefully complimented the project for teaching them research skills and about the world they live in, and about valuing newspaper reading. Many students also evidence artistic skills. This project will last them a lifetime. Their course grade also prospers, because these projects often well exceed 100 points for extra effort. (In recent semesters for logistical reasons, I've scaled down the project parameters as follows: one article/paragraph about Global Interdependence; a Sociology concept of their interest; a Multinational Corporation. Each article has to be mounted, titled, explained and applied to the course, and documented to the textbook and newspaper source. Again, the campus library supplies weeded newspapers.

D.R. Wilson
Houston Baptist University
IRM for Kendall's Sociology in Our Times: The Essentials, 5E, p. 346

These are just a few of the sites on the Internet dealing with riots. Conduct a more extensive search for historical accounts and news stories of riots here in the U.S. and around the world.

1) The 1943 Detroit Race Riots
http://detnews.com/history/riot/riot.htm;
2) Riots in Haiti
http://crawfurd.dk/africa/haiti200.htm;
3) 1966-77 Riots in Chicago
http://www.chipublib.org/004chicago/disasters/riots_1966to 1977.html;
4) Borneo Riots
http://www.cnn.com/WORLD/asiapcf/9903/21/indonesia. borneo/

CPSIA information can be obtained
at www.ICGtesting.com
Printed in the USA
FFOW022120050413
1076FF